Contents

Contents

CONTENTS

Les Brown

INTRODUCTION

"Men may not get all they pay for in this world, but they must certainly pay for all they get."
—Frederick Douglass, former slave and abolitionist

When I look at my life—from my birth in an abandoned building and my upbringing in Liberty City, the poor area of Miami, Florida; from being labeled "educable mentally retarded" to speaking to corporations, organizations and audiences around the world, including over eighty thousand people in the Georgia Dome—every dream I've ever realized required a fight.

The desire to get out of Liberty City; to take care of my mother, Mrs. Mamie Brown, and buy her a home; to live on a larger scale; to travel the world; to touch people's lives; to be a force for good— all of that required me to fight. Every step of the way, it has been a struggle to advance myself—which is why I chose to title this, my first collection of inspirational stories, *Fight For Your Dreams*.

The individuals who so courageously and humbly agreed to share their very personal stories in this book represent all of us who have this universal desire to live the greatest version of who we are. I admire them for their unstoppable spirit, because through their example you will be reminded of your own dreams—the dreams you keep close to your heart and act on every day, the dreams you put away long ago, the dreams that still call to you, begging to be fulfilled. Your dream is worth the fight. Your dream is not frivolous, or even optional. Your dream is necessary.

You have something special. You have greatness within you. You have something no one else has: some idea; some invention; some cause, message or movement; a unique voice, idea or kind of leadership. You have something the world *needs,* and if you don't bring it out, we will all be deprived.

To prove to you that you have something special, let me remind you that you were chosen, one out of four hundred million sperm.

> *Your dream is worth the fight. Your dream is not frivolous, or even optional. Your dream is necessary.*

You stood out in the eyes of God. He chose you and put in you something that needed to be produced and expressed on this earth plane, and it is mandatory that you do whatever is required to make sure that you complete your mission. Greatness is not your destiny. Greatness is a choice you make each and every day.

To be successful, you must ward off the inner demons of mediocrity, fear, lack of self-confidence—all of your internal obstacles and challenges, as well as your external challenges. To do this, you must be at your best at all times. You must be willing to go to the center of the ring and fight to achieve the things that will give your life a sense of meaning, purpose and value.

To manifest your greatness, you must immerse yourself in an ongoing process of self-awareness, self-approval, self-commitment and self-fulfillment. Transforming your life requires dying to who you are now and giving birth to whom you must become. It's going to take everything in you to be focused and disciplined and to keep the faith. It will be the most challenging experience you will ever have. Perhaps that's why Shakespeare wrote, in his play *Julius Caesar,* "The fault, dear Brutus, is not in the stars, but in ourselves that we are underlings." We live in a world where we are constantly being criticized and made to feel as though we don't matter. This creates a level of cynicism, frustration and hopelessness. We end up going through life with a limited vision and living as volunteer victims.

In the process of self-discovery, you will meet internal and external opposition that will challenge your faith and your resolve. You might receive a fatal diagnosis, or something may happen to someone you care about, or you may literally have your life as you know it snatched out from under you. In some cases family members and friends will turn against you, and you will begin to doubt yourself. However, I can tell you based upon my own experience that, in spite of those things, you have something special. You have greatness in you. You are greater than your circumstances, or anything that you have ever experienced or are facing right now.

I have a saying: "If life knocks you down, try to land on your back, because if you can look up, you can get up." You have greatness within you, and the canvas is no place for your greatness. You have comeback power! The greatest power that God has given you is the power to choose—to surrender, or to stand up inside yourself and fight. Yet remember, if you do what is easy, your life will be hard. However, if you do what is hard, your life will be easy.

I can tell you straight up that it's going to be hard to make it through life and fight through the challenges. Thinking positively and being enthusiastic when life slaps you upside the head is not easy. It's going to be hard—really hard—to stay positive. It's hard taking care of aging parents, raising children, being a part of the sandwich generation and simultaneously managing a career. It's hard picking up the pieces, starting over again when you've lost your retirement or find yourself upside-down in your mortgage. It's hard when your spouse wakes up one morning after years of marriage and says, "I don't want to be married anymore, at least not to you."

It's hard when you've given the best years of your life to your children and they don't appreciate or value the sacrifices you made, don't understand the price you paid to get to where you are right now. It's hard when you become sick; when the doctor looks at you and says that they've done all that they can do and there's no hope—and there you are, lying on your back, and all you have to hang onto is your faith. It's hard when people who should be there for you—loving you, encouraging you and motivating you—not only refuse to raise a hand to help you, but literally turn against you out of jealousy and envy, out of hope you will fail.

It's hard to keep your spirits up when you cannot see the light at the end of the tunnel. But I believe my good friend Willie Jolley was right when he said that a setback is a set-up for a comeback. My favorite book says, "Think it not strange that ye face the fiery furnaces of this world." You will face trials and tribulations. When this happens, it could be easy to quit, to point at your circumstances to justify why you didn't make it. It's easy to come up with excuses and to complain. It would be easy to just roll over and play dead; to turn to drugs or alcohol and just throw in the towel on yourself and your dreams. But remember, if you do what is easy, your life will be hard. However, if you do what is hard, your life will be easy.

I procrastinated for fourteen years. I didn't pursue my dreams because I was afraid. I used the excuse that I was poor; that I was labeled educable mentally retarded; that I was called DT, the "dumb twin;" that I failed in school twice and that I had no college training. I had built a strong case for why I couldn't pursue my dreams or live a life of greatness. But I realize that Ralph Waldo Emerson was right when he said, "What lies before you and what lies behind is of small consequence to what lies within you."

We live our lives as a result of the story we believe about ourselves and the things we say to ourselves. By reading the stories in this book, all of which are testaments to the power of never giving up, you will begin to transform your mindset and expand your vision beyond your mental conditioning and your circumstances. Reading these stories will take you to a place within yourself where greatness lives. Reading these stories will create a spark, a desire and a hunger within you to answer the call and challenge yourself to live an extraordinary life.

To paraphrase US Supreme Court Justice Oliver Wendell Holmes, "Once a man's or woman's mind has been expanded by a new idea, concept or story, it can never be satisfied by going back to where it was." After reading these triumphant stories of dreams once dashed and now fulfilled, of heartbreak and undying love, of

> *What is possible for one is possible for all.*

inner demons vanquished and obstacles tossed aside, your mind and your life will never go back to where they were.

What is possible for one is possible for all. When we simply see examples of other people's success, we are inspired to take responsibility to do what we know in our heart of hearts we CAN do. It's not going to be easy. Sometimes your path will be so arduous that you will want to give up. But it will be worth it.

Each story in this book will inspire the still, small voice within you to say, "If they can do it, I can do it." Each chapter will inspire you to get out of the bleachers of life and come out onto the field to play a bigger game. Each page will remind you that you have greatness within you, and that it's not over until you win. It is not an accident that you are reading this book at this time. I've come to believe that things don't just happen; they happen for a reason. When I look back on my life, every person I met, every experience I had and every book I read played some role in influencing how I saw myself and what I believed was possible for me. I invite you to pause for a moment in reflection and say to yourself, "This is my time."

Affirm with conviction, "This book is going to change my life." Think about three major goals that you would like to achieve in your personal life, in your financial life and in your social contribution. Then, make up your mind that you will reach the majority of your goals. Write down five reasons why you will not give up on yourself, or on your dreams. Your reasons will give you the strength, the emotional stamina and the courage to keep on keeping on when everything tells you to stop.

The great philosopher Friedrich Nietzsche once said, "If you know the why for living, you can endure almost any how." Your reasons will be your rod and staff to comfort you during the challenging moments. Your reasons will provide you with the mental resiliency to keep on keeping on swinging and slugging it out, to fight the good fight. Your reasons will inspire you to become, as Mother Teresa said, "a pencil in the hand of God," and start writing new chapters with your life.

Les Brown

BE WILLING TO PAY THE PRICE

I pride myself on being able to do more push-ups than any of my five sons. At the age of sixty-six, I'm able to do more than one-hundred-forty-two consecutive push-ups. I couldn't do that when I was fifteen, or twenty, or twenty-five. It's not a thing to brag about when you think about legendary fitness expert Jack LaLanne, who could do more than a thousand push-ups in less than half an hour!

One day, while playing with some of the members of my audience, challenging myself to do push-ups, I felt a pain in my back that I'd never felt before. The pain felt like an axe in my back. It stayed with me, and even after a series of massages and acupuncture and chiropractic treatments, the pain was an ever-present feeling. Thinking I had a pinched nerve or some other chronic issue, my business partner, Dr. Julie VanPutten, urged me to see a doctor.

As a fourteen-year prostate cancer conqueror, I had been vigilant about going to the doctor for checkups, bone scans and soft tissue scans—in short, all that was required of a one-time cancer patient. Because of this, I felt there was no need to go. So I waited. For months, I lived with sometimes excruciating pain. Eventually I agreed to be examined, and submitted myself to more tests and scans.

Julie, who had a personal relationship with the physician, Dr. Frank Stone, looked at the scans and talked with him. Looking at her face, I could tell she was trying to conceal her feelings and emotions. She knew something. I'm sure that you've had the experience of watching a person's energy shift when they tell you nothing's wrong. You cannot put your finger on it, but you feel that there's something they are holding back. I confronted her and said, "Tell me. I need to know. I can handle it."

She said sadly, "You have cancer on your spine. You have to go back to the doctor tomorrow morning to discuss the treatment plan." After hearing those words, I monitored my feelings. I didn't really feel anything. That night I laid in bed thinking about

> *It takes persistence, perseverance and a fighting spirit to achieve anything you want in life.*

how I was going to deal with this. It was my second time around. What was I going to do with this next fight that threatened my dreams and my life?

When we returned to the Dr. Stone's office, I came in as "Mr. Motivator," laughing and talking. I decided: *I will beat the cancer on my spine like I beat prostate cancer the first time.* When I sat down, I said to Dr. Stone, "I know that I have cancer on the spine. So what do you suggest?" He shocked me out of my wits when he said, "Mr. Brown, you have cancer on your spine. You also have cancer on your right collarbone, your rib cage, and your pelvic area, and you have a cyst on your liver. All together, we have identified eight different areas of metastasized prostate cancer throughout your body."

I started laughing. The doctor, who had braced himself for an entirely different reaction, said, "Why are you laughing?" Still chuckling, I answered, "I feel like Mother Teresa right now." "What do you mean?" he asked. I told him that Mother Teresa once said, "Lord, I know you know how much I can bear. I just wish you didn't have so much confidence in me."

We both laughed, and then we proceeded to talk about a treatment strategy, my options, and new advances in traditional and alternative medicine. I'd been down this path before. The words "metastasized prostate cancer" meant I was in for the fight for my life. Cancer is the most feared word in seven different languages. "You have cancer" are three words that no one ever wants to hear.

> When life throws you a curveball, knock it out of the park.

The first time I heard my own diagnosis of cancer fourteen years ago, I was most definitely shocked and frightened. I couldn't believe it. At that time I was preparing to do a radio campaign on the WBLS station in New York City, where I worked as a morning host, to convince men to take their prostate examinations. I realized that, at the age of fifty-two, I had never had a prostate examination myself. I decided to have the examination so that I could properly advise others, and discovered during that first-ever examination that I had prostate cancer. I was *traumatized*. I remember thinking, *Oh my God, I'm going to die,* because that's the prevailing conversation about cancer in our culture.

When most people hear the word "cancer," they consciously or unconsciously believe that they've just been given a death sentence, and that's how I received the news the first time around.

Not this time. Sitting in Dr. Stone's office, I checked my body for signs of fear, but I felt nothing. I had just been told I had cancer in eight different areas of my body, and I felt *no fear,* no nervousness, and no anxiety. I sat in the doctor's office, feeling confident and thinking, *I can handle this. I can kick cancer's butt—again.* I told the doctor, "I've been down this road before. I've fought this battle. I won then, and I'm prepared to win now." Julie looked at me and said, "Les, you *are* going to beat this." I had beaten cancer so badly the first time that cancer wanted a rematch.

9

When I look at life, I know that it's about the willingness to stand up; the willingness to fight for what you want; and the willingness not to deny a disease, hardship or circumstance but, rather, to defy it. It takes persistence, perseverance and a fighting spirit to achieve anything you want in life. Wilson Pickett had a song called, "99 ½ Won't Do It, You Have To Have 100." A.L.

> *You must fight for your dreams as if your life depends on it, because it does.*

Williams, entrepreneur and motivational speaker, used to motivate his staff by saying, "All you can do is all you can do, and all you can do is enough. But make sure you do all you can do."

When life throws you a curveball, knock it out of the park. When the doctor informed me that I would have to take up the charge and fight cancer again, he said, "The cancer has eaten forty percent of your T-1 vertebra. I don't know how you've been able to handle the pain this long." He looked at me in awe, and despite his practiced professional veneer, he looked quite concerned. Studies indicate that more people die from the doctor's prognosis than from the disease itself. Gazing at my doctor, I borrowed a line from Philippe Petit, a tightrope walker who, as documented in the movie *Man on Wire,* strung a rope between the World Trade Center's Twin Towers in New York City and walked it. I said to myself, *This is impossible… Let's get started.*

It is critical that you believe in yourself. Most people don't have the courage or the willingness to say "yes" to their dreams, much less to stand up and fight for them. This is partly because society tells us to focus on our limitations rather than on our potential. Eighty-seven percent of Americans go to jobs they hate. In the United States, the heart attack rate increases by thirty-five percent on Monday mornings between the hours of six and ten. The majority of these stressed out, fear-driven individuals die on the toilet, getting ready to go to work someplace they hate. They focus on their limitations, rather than their possibilities, and then curl up and die. You must fight for your dreams as if your life depends on it, because it does.

It has been said that the two most important moments in our lives are the day we were born, and the day we realized why we were born. Your dreams matter. My friend Joelle Martin once said, "What would the world be like if everyone lived their dreams?"

After years of doing seminars and workshops, and having the opportunity to hear people talk about their dreams—finding cures for cancer, ending world suffering, poverty, wars, hunger

> *What you become in pursuit of your dream is more important than the accomplishment of your dream.*

and homelessness—I believe that dreams are from God, and all of us are sent here with an assignment to make our dreams become reality, to make the world a better place.

The great theologian and civil rights leader Howard Thurman, mentor to Dr. Martin Luther King, Jr., Mahatma Gandhi and other leaders said, "There is something in every one of you that waits and listens for the voice of the genuine in yourself. It is the only true guide you will ever have. And if you cannot hear it, you will all of your life spend your days on the ends of strings that somebody else pulls." Whatever you were called to do, whatever this "something" is for you, whatever your "genuine" is, you must draw your own line in the sand, take up the challenge and fight, fight, fight for your dream.

As I said in the introduction, fighting for your dreams is not easy. We can predict the outcome of some dreams, but most of the time, *a dream has a life of its own.* When will a baby walk? He will walk when he walks. When will a baby talk? She will talk when she talks. We seldom know the day or the hour that our dreams will come true, which can make the whole thing seem just a bit *too* hard. We do all of this work pushing past comfort zones, setting aside fears, slaying inner demons, recommitting to the goal every day, every single day, and we *still* don't know when it will come to fruition. And most of the time, I can tell you based upon my own experience, you will fail your way to success. Make failure your friend. It will happen—but remember this: What you become in pursuit of your dream is more important than the accomplishment of your dream.

My son, John-Leslie, who is a positive hip-hop artist known as "High Hopes," once asked me, "What if I don't reach my dream?" I said to him, "There is power in the *pursuit* of your dream."

I found out that achieving your dream is not the most important thing. Oddly enough, the most important thing is the person you become while in pursuit of your dream—your character development; your spirituality, courage and faith; the experiences you have along the way, good and bad; and the relationships you develop. All these things come together to create a new you. The pursuit introduces you to a part of yourself that you didn't know before, because you have now become willing to put yourself in a perpetual state of discomfort; and that is the key to winning the battle for developing your greatness and living your dream.

You have greatness within you. If you are willing to take life on, to go to the center of the ring and face it with your head up, and to slug it out, you will develop your greatness and live your dream. I'm reminded of the words from the poem *Invictus* by William Ernest Henley:

Out of the night that covers me,
Black as the Pit from pole to pole,
I thank whatever gods may be
For my unconquerable soul.

In the fell clutch of circumstance
I have not winced nor cried aloud.
Under the bludgeonings of chance
My head is bloody, but unbowed.

Beyond this place of wrath and tears
Looms but the Horror of the shade,
And yet the menace of the years
Finds, and shall find, me unafraid.

It matters not how strait the gate,
How charged with punishments the scroll,
I am the master of my fate:
I am the captain of my soul.

Les Brown is a distinguished authority on harnessing human potential. A top motivational speaker, an extraordinary speech coach, and the bestselling author of Live Your Dreams, It's Not Over Till You Win *and* Up Thoughts for Down Times, *his passionate, straight-from-the-heart message motivates audiences to create a larger vision for their lives and to fight for their dreams. Born in an abandoned building in Liberty City, Florida, and raised in poverty, Brown rose from a hip-talking morning DJ to become a thrice-elected State Representative in Ohio, and then an award-winning, premier keynote speaker for Fortune 500 companies and for organizations worldwide. He is the recipient of the National Speaker Association's highest honors, the Council of Peers Award of Excellence. He also received the highest award from Toastmasters International, The Golden Gavel Award. Toastmasters International separately named him one of the top five speakers in the world. His PBS program* You Deserve *was awarded a Chicago-area Emmy. Brown is now a radio personality at KFWB NewsTalk 980 AM in Los Angeles. He is also a communication and speech consultant who teaches people how to unwrap their "infinite greatness." Connect with Les at www.LesBrown.com and email him your personal success story.*

Shaune B. Arnold, Esq.

FIGHT ON

The phone fairly buzzed with the sound of my father's angry voice. "Did you get the note?" My blood ran cold. "I'm sorry, Dad. I forgot." "You're in trouble," he said, darkly, and hung up.

In this life you play the hand you hold. So what do you do when the deck is stacked against you? Born government-issue, in Sai-Tama Ken, Japan, I spent my first eight years of life on Air Force bases abroad and stateside. Growing up, our parents taught my sister and me many wonderful things. We were respectful of our elders and peers, well traveled, and each developed a voracious thirst for knowledge. Unfortunately, though, from the beginning, there were terrible cracks in the veneer of our lives.

There was a lot of violence in the household. I never knew when it would erupt, but when it did there would sometimes, quite literally, be blood on the walls. It had always been that way. On my fifth birthday, before I blew out the candles on my cake, I wished I could belong to a different family.

When I was thirteen my father, now retired from the service, graduated from Harvard Law School, and we all moved to New York City, taking up residence on Roosevelt Island. I went to school on the island. The transition to a new school and new culture was difficult. The East River flowed along both sides of the small island community, isolating us from Manhattan and Queens. It felt claustrophobic to my teenage spirit.

Some classes were harder for me than others. I received a poor grade on a social studies research project. Like any self-respecting teenager I blamed the scarcity of materials in the tiny one-room library on the island. My father and teacher agreed that I could do

> *On my fifth birthday, before I blew out the candles on my cake, I wished I could belong to a different family.*

the project again using materials from a library in Manhattan. In order to do so I had to get a school note identifying me as a student on the island. I was only too happy to comply as I was very excited about the prospect of going into *The City* on my own!

However, the following day the test results were released from all of the specialized high schools in New York City. I had taken several of the entrance exams, and was excited and distracted by the news of the various schools that had and had not accepted me. *I completely forgot to get the note.*

As usual, that day, I let myself into the house and did my chores, all timed to be completed just as my parents got home—their way of knowing that my sister and I were home on time and staying out of trouble. My father called at the appointed hour. I started excitedly telling him about my test results. He didn't care. All he cared about was whether I got the note. I knew before he said it that I was in deep trouble.

He got home from work at about ten at night, yanked me out of bed by my curlers and dragged me upstairs. By the time he was finished with me, I had a black eye, a split lip and a hairline fracture on my left arm. As my mother covered my wounds with makeup the next day before school, she said, "You asked for it. If you had just gotten the letter, you wouldn't have gotten into trouble." She was not my ally.

That morning in class, two thoughts occurred to me. The first was: *If you had to put makeup on me so I could go to school, you knew it was wrong.* The second was: *Either my father or I will not physically survive my childhood. One of us is not going to make it.* I was growing into a person—I was growing into a woman. The woman I was becoming simply could not take another beating.

Still in shock, I went home for lunch. Instead of eating, I sat for a while in silence. I had no specific intent to call anyone, but somehow, the phone found its way into my hand. I called the police. The desk sergeant answered the phone. "Sir," I said. "I need to know what constitutes child abuse according to the law." He said, "Well, hitting a child so as to leave a mark." I glanced down at the purple bruise on my swollen arm. He continued, "Not clothing that child, not feeding that child. And there's such a thing as emotional abuse, as well."

I gathered my courage and found my voice. "I think I need to report a case of child abuse."

"Are you a teacher? A neighbor?" "No, I'm the child," I replied. "Oh, no," he stated matter-of-factly. "You have to be under age eighteen." "I'm fourteen," I responded. "You're fourteen?!" He

> *I believed my life was on the line. I was without a family, and living in group homes where no one truly expected me to succeed.*

couldn't believe I was so young (I was a rather cerebral child). The policeman asked me a few more questions. I explained what had happened and described my injuries. In the distance the school bell rang, summoning me back to class. He asked for my phone number. "The bell just rang. I have to go back to school, or I'm going to get in trouble!" "Give me your phone number and don't you move!" he commanded. I complied with his order.

He called back in less than two minutes. "I want you to get on the train and go to the Bureau of Child Welfare. They're waiting for you." "I can't, sir. I don't have any money." We lived in a two-story apartment in the middle of New York City, my father was a Harvard graduate, and I was dead broke. The officer told me to go to school and borrow the money from the principal's office. I said that I would, and hung up. Summoning all of my strength, I went down to my bedroom, and put a few articles of clothing in a little beach bag. Then, walking solemnly up the stairs, I left my parents' home for the last time.

The social worker called my parents to tell them I was in the hospital and that I had made charges against them. Their response was simply, "Keep her. We don't want her." Three months later, I found myself suing my parents for divorce. The court battle

> *I instinctively understood that shaking my fist at the sky was no longer necessary, but it took me a while to stop swinging at empty air.*

spanned a number of years, and my family was never the same again. My parents and I, and in a lot of ways even my sister and I, squared off against one another. I believed my life was on the line. I was without a family, and living in group homes where no one truly expected me to succeed.

The family reunification services ordered by the court were ineffective at best. Our familial wounds only festered over time. At one meeting my father shouted, "Without me, you'll be a sixteen-year-old pregnant whore on the streets of New York City!" Having been raised very close to the vest, I was quite naïve about a lot of things, and still very shy.

However, after nearly two years free of his abuse, my voice had only grown stronger. I glared back at him steadily. "I'm going to shove your Harvard Law School education right up your ass! Watch me and see if I don't." That exchange ended our family reunification meetings.

Shortly thereafter my parents moved to California, leaving me alone in New York. Now just seventeen years old, I was completely alone. In those early days I developed a deep resolve to make it through the tough times. I nurtured the tender embers of a vision for my life, one in which I would be free of pain and crippling depression, where I would attend college and eventually control my own destiny. Admittedly, in those early days, my resolve was firmly rooted in my ego. Too many people who should have been cheering me on would revel in my fall. I was not going to give them that grim pleasure. I dug into my schoolwork and applied to college because it was my best chance of escape. *I know I have a right to an education and a better life.*

When I lifted my head I had attained a Bachelor of Arts degree in psychology from the University of California, Los Angeles, and a Juris Doctorate from the University of California's Hastings College of the Law. The day I walked across the stage to receive my doctorate was the happiest day of my life—I felt light of spirit. However, taking the California Bar Exam brought its own set of struggles.

> *As a girl I knew I had the right to live and live fully, no matter who said otherwise. As a woman I know I have a right to happiness, love, and inner peace. This is the vision that I hold for my present and for my future.*

I took the bar exam several times, as did many of my friends. As time wore on some of them gave up, but I just couldn't. To me, the failure wasn't in repeatedly taking the bar exam. Rather, it would have been in giving up. I dug deeper and persisted until I passed the exam. In my mind, on that day I effectively buried *his* Harvard Law School education right where the sun don't shine. On that day, the years of anger and depression dissipated. I instinctively understood that shaking my fist at the sky was no longer necessary, but it took me a while to stop swinging at empty air. *Rest now. You've done well, my dear.*

In retrospect, I believe that a lot of my inner turmoil was unnecessary. The universe put me right where it wanted me to be. I liken my family's situation to the story of David in the Bible. David loved God, and God loved David; but David sent a woman's husband to the front lines to be killed because he coveted her. Due to this transgression, David was not allowed to build the Temple of God. This task fell to his son, Solomon. Likewise, the only thing my father ever wanted was to go to Harvard Law School and be a lawyer. He graduated from Harvard, but never passed a bar exam. The transgression he committed by sowing violence into his family may have prevented him from building his temple. That task fell to his daughter.

As a child, I fought for my life when I made the call that changed everything, and then divorced my parents. Holding fast to my vision of attending college, I pulled it deep within my heart and protected it from harm. I meditated on it. I persisted and banked everything on it, and, in so doing, I developed the flexibility to handle life's challenges. Whatever those challenges were, they could not displace my vision for my life. When faced with an issue, I would put the challenge into perspective. If I couldn't go through it, over it or under it, I would find a way around it. Education would be my ticket to freedom. *No matter what.*

As a girl I knew I had the right to live and live fully, no matter who said otherwise. As a woman I know I have a right to happiness, love, and inner peace. This is the vision that I hold for my present and for my future. People give up on their dreams when they think they don't have a right to them. You must understand on a cellular level that you *do* have a right to your dreams, even if they are hard to achieve. You may *have to fight for your dreams,* even as you'd fight for your life. You must decide that your dreams are worth the struggle. *Fight on,* even if the struggle leaves your ego bloodied, battered, and bruised. *Get up off your knees,* even if you must stand alone. *Do it again, and again, and again... until, at last, you succeed.*

Shaune B. Arnold, Esq. is a practicing transaction attorney in Los Angeles, California. A member of MENSA, and a graduate of UCLA and the University of California Hastings College of the Law, she is also a former licensed Financial Advisor, holding Series 7, Series 63, Series 65 and Insurance licenses for several years. As an entrepreneur, Shaune is General Counsel and CEO of The Book Factory, Inc., a full-service publishing company. Also, drawing on her seventeen years of business law practice, Shaune has developed a twelve-week Hardcore Business Boot Camp for entrepreneurs, taking them all the way from conceptualizing a business and drafting a winning business plan, to branding, operating, marketing and ultimately profiting from a successful business. Connect with Shaune at www.BusinessBootCampOnline.com.

Allen P. Cardoza

THE MAGIC WAND

I t was a breezy summer night, and I was sitting in my car, staking out what I thought was a party. I'd been hired by a frantic mother to find her runaway daughter, and all my developed leads led me to this particular house, a typical, middle-income house in a decent residential neighborhood. I thought it was a party because teenage girls kept arriving and going inside.

I'd been doing investigative work for a year, but I'd only recently begun tracking down runaways. "I'm going to send you out to find these runaways because you look like them," my boss, Walt, had told me. By that he meant I was young—like them. I was nineteen years old at the time. The girl I was looking for was fifteen. I was a little bored, sitting and staring at a house through binoculars, but I was being persistent. When Walt hired me, he'd said, "To do this job, you need to be part salesman, part con man and part psychologist, and the only people who succeed in this industry are those who are really persistent."

Some older men started to arrive at the house, and I figured the party was about to break up. I assumed the men arriving were the fathers of the girls inside. One guy with a pot belly and thinning hair, probably in his early fifties, showed up and walked out with a girl who looked like the child I was looking for. The mother who hired me told me that her ex-husband was on board and that once

I found their daughter, they'd work together to put her into a drug rehab program.

I immediately assumed that the father was trying to please both sides on this and that he was harboring his daughter while pretending to help his ex-wife find her. I'd seen enough nasty divorces with parents lying to each other, so this didn't surprise me. They got into his car and drove off, and I followed them so that I could report to the mother that her daughter was okay.

When they ended up in a trailer park, something didn't seem right. I got out of my car and walked up to the trailer they'd entered. Inside, the older man was having sex with the girl. I was

> This is my calling, *I thought immediately. I knew I needed to locate young people, help them, talk to them, work with them. From that moment on, I knew what I would be doing for the rest of my life.*

confused, devastated and disgusted. I went back to the office and told Walt what was happening. "This isn't an isolated incident," he said. "It's called human trafficking, and it happens all the time."

This is my calling, I thought immediately. I knew I needed to locate young people, help them, talk to them, work with them. From that moment on, I knew what I would be doing for the rest of my life. I was so new to this world of abuse and exploitation that I didn't even understand the terminology. Trafficking? I had no idea what it meant. But I soon learned.

That was thirty years ago, and since then I have worked with or transported over sixteen-thousand teenagers. Yes, sixteen thousand. It's an amazing number, but it's a drop in the bucket. 2007 statistics show that one in seven kids between the ages of ten and eighteen will run away at some point, and there are currently one to three million runaway teens in the United States.

Soon after that first illuminating conversation with Walt, I found the girl we were hired to find and placed her in a program where she could get help. I also brought in law enforcement to bust up the trafficking ring. Until that moment, I'd never really helped another human being to that extent. Before becoming an investigator, I'd worked in the family roofing business. Two herniated discs from a nasty fall off of a roof changed my career trajectory—for which I am eternally grateful!

Even so, that first year, most of the private investigation work didn't feel like a calling. I was doing car repossessions, tracking down cheating wives, that kind of thing, and while it was fun, it wasn't particularly gratifying. These kids, though, they were something worth fighting for—really fighting for. They were worth early mornings and late nights and turning over every stone, because lives were at stake, young lives with so much potential—if they could only be rescued in time.

I had another trafficking case in Holland. A fifteen-year-old girl had run away. After spending weeks looking for her, I finally located her in a club where you picked out a girl, paid a fee, took her where you wanted and brought her back when finished. I paid

> In the hotel room, the other agent and I showed this girl a picture of her family, and a video of her family telling her they loved and missed her. "We're here to free you," we told her.

for the girl, and took her to a hotel room where I had another investigator, a female, waiting. In the hotel room, the other agent and I showed this girl a picture of her family, and a video of her family telling her they loved and missed her. "We're here to free you," we told her.

When you take girls from this club, a bouncer follows you to make sure you bring her back. We were definitely followed—I saw the guy standing outside, across the street—but I'd already worked it out with the police to pick him up. The girl was crying, saying she couldn't go with us.

"Of course you can go with us," I said. "I've got police ready to come and pick up that bouncer."

The girl shook her head, crying. She showed us a picture of one of her siblings sighted through a riflescope with crosshairs. "If I go with you," she said, "they will kill this sister. And they said they will take my other one, my younger sister, and replace me in the club with her. I can't go with you."

We took her back to the club. I had to figure out a way to bust this girl free. I felt sick to my stomach leaving that club without her.

We moved the girl's family to a discreet location and shot another video of them to assure the girl they were safe. Weeks later, I went back to the club, paid for the same girl and took her to the same hotel. I showed her the video of her family, and she wept again, but this time with tears of joy. I called in local law enforcement to pick up the bouncer who followed us, and I put the girl on a plane back to her family.

Over time I have developed a unique ability to work with these troubled teens. The secret is to ask the right questions with empathy, so they don't think they're being interrogated, and *really* listen to their answers! I ask them what brought them to this point. I also ask what I can do to serve them.

"Let's say I have a magic wand," I say. "If I could wave this magic wand and make your wish come true, what is the first thing you'd want me to do?" "Make Dad quit drinking," one might say. "Make my parents listen to me more," another says. "Tell Mom to quit taking Valium™." "Make the bullies at school leave me alone." These are pretty typical responses. When you start a conversation by asking these kids what they want, they'll tell you what's really going on.

As word of my love for working with these troubled teens traveled, I started getting hired to go to the homes of parents and help escort their kids to rehab facilities, boarding schools and residential treatment centers. I even wrote a manual that addresses not only how to locate troubled teens who have run away but also how to talk to them in such a way that they feel safe and know you truly care.

The work pays off in so many ways. A few years ago, at Thanksgiving, I was seated at the table with my extended family. They still had the family construction business, and for years I tried to make them understand the importance of what I do, but I still thought they just didn't see it the same way I did. During the meal, my cell phone rang. My family seemed perturbed that I worked on holidays, but a ringing phone could mean a client in distress.

I excused myself, went into another room and answered. After I said hello, a voice said, "You probably don't remember me, but my name is Jeff." I told him that of course I remembered him; thirteen

> *That's what I do. I help people realize their dreams—people for whom dreams seem impossible. And a huge way I can realize* my *dreams is to help someone else fully realize her own.*

years before I'd located and transported him. He went on to say that he was at his own Thanksgiving table with his own multi-generational family, and as they ate, they went around the table saying what each was thankful for.

"I said I was thankful for you," he said. "My parents were my parents. Of course they didn't give up on finding me and straightening me out. But you were a stranger. And not only did you not give up on me, you cared enough to tell me never to give up on myself." He was now married and had a career, and his wife was pregnant with their first child. He called because his family said he should. He called to say thanks.

That's what I do. I help people realize their dreams—people for whom dreams seem impossible. And a huge way I can realize *my* dreams is to help someone else fully realize her own. I went back to my own family's Thanksgiving table in tears. I told them about the phone call. I told them about how I'd initially located this boy and gotten him into a treatment program. I told them how he ran away from that program, twice, and how both times I found him and brought him back. I then told them about his life today. I think they finally understood why I do what I do.

I do fight for dreams, the dreams of "at risk" children. And by fighting for their dreams, I'm fighting for mine. That's how you've got to fight for your dreams—as if they're the dreams of a child, your child. You have to endure the early mornings and late nights, and you have to turn over every stone out there. But first, you have to find that dream. So, let me ask: if I could wave a magic wand and grant you a wish, one wish, what would it be?

Allen Cardoza is a licensed private investigator (PI 7824) and an instructor of non-violent crisis intervention. He is the founder and president of West Shield Investigations, which has successfully located and, through its partner company Adolescent Services, Inc., returned thousands of runaway children to homes, hospitals and schools for over twenty-five years. Allen also hosts a weekly radio talk show geared toward giving advice to families in crisis, Answers for the Family. *(www.Answers4TheFamilyblog.com). Through his speeches, articles and forthcoming book,* Running Away in America, *Allen offers solutions for parents and teens, and sheds light on the human trafficking epidemic. Connect with Allen at www.WestShield.com and www.TransportingTeens. com.*

Alisa Gabrielle

A Life You Love

Standing before the enormous, vibrant canvases, I am enthralled. Heart pounding, my whole being lights up. Breathless, I move from one painting to the next and back again. Each canvas is a new story that seems to speak directly to me. I am ten years old, and I have fallen in love with art.

"Look at the brush strokes, Mommy, and the colors. They're so powerful," I say, admiring a Van Gogh. My ability to put words to my impressions surprises both of us. I just cannot stop talking to her about the work. Miro's bright reds and glowing blues mesmerize me; his black, playful lines make me smile. Gauguin's exquisite palette and native scenes touch my heart. My eyes well up with tears. And then, I offer up a silent prayer, a wish: *I want to become a great artist.*

That visit to my first art exhibition changed my life. My soul was speaking to me, though I didn't know it at the time. I remember thinking, *I would love to create beautiful art that gives people the same feeling of delight and overwhelming joy I feel now.* (Yes, even at the age of ten, I longed for that.) I didn't really believe I could actually *become* an artist, but my mother, who adored me, offered to send me to art classes.

I took an oil painting class with an instructor whose methods were too sophisticated for children. I left uninspired. I tried drawing bodies and faces on my own, but they were not very realistic. At that point I made a judgment that altered the course of my life: *I'm not good enough to be an artist. If Mozart could compose music at age five, and I can't draw correctly by age ten, I must not be meant to be an artist,* I reasoned. I killed my dream right there on the spot... or so I thought.

I followed other dreams I had early on, first of teaching, and then of helping people live more satisfying lives, which I did as a Marriage and Family Therapist. But the artist in me remained unfulfilled. I began to use crayons and clay to help my clients

> *I wanted more—I wanted to live a life I* loved.

express what words often could not. I collected paintings and sculptures I bought at local art shows, and took a few art history classes. Still, it was not enough to fulfill my longing.

After many years in practice, I began to burn out. Along with a huge caseload, I was running my own counseling center, supervising a large staff, training interns and hosting weekly radio and cable TV shows. But it was more than burnout. Underneath the exhaustion, my soul beckoned. I realized, *I've been encouraging and helping my clients to live their dreams, but I'm not living mine.* I longed to go to Europe, live like a local in a small town and study art. I loved Italy—the art, architecture, language and, of course, the food!

I wanted more—I wanted to live a life I *loved.* I sold my counseling center and took some time off. I thought, *I'm going to focus on what I enjoy—art—even if it's only for a short time.* I finally got up the courage to take two art classes, but my bigger dream, the dream of becoming an artist, still lay dormant. Eventually I resumed my practice, albeit at a slower pace. One day I shared what I longed to do with my manicurist. She told me her sister had taken a marble-carving class in Italy. She added, "Her instructor teaches sculpting right nearby." Was it luck, or providence? Excited, I went to meet her sister. She raved about her experience carving stone in a wonderful little town called Pietrasanta. Even though I had no desire to work in marble, I decided to meet the teacher.

Bernice, a large white-haired woman with an even larger personality, greeted me warmly and showed me to her studio. I wanted to leave immediately. The noise from the air compressors and tools carving against stone was irritatingly loud. The air was filled with stone dust, and the students, dressed in sloppy overalls, were covered in it from head to toe. Struggling to breathe, I thought, *this is not what I had in mind.* "Here!" Bernice said, plunking the heavy vibrating air hammer and chisel in my hands. I thought, *That looks dangerous!* I gasped. "I do *not* do tools! Would you consider teaching me in clay, instead?" It was more like begging than asking, but she agreed.

"When are you leaving for Italy?" I asked. "In three weeks," she replied casually. *Three weeks!* I panicked. *What am I going to tell my clients?* I knew that if I were gone for months I might lose the practice I had just rebuilt. The expenses for the trip, studio, tools and hotel alone were daunting. It was a HUGE risk to leave everything behind—my home, my pets, life as I knew it—just to make some art that would probably end up in my garage. *This is your one chance to live your dream.* I blurted out, "Okay. Sign me up… as long as I don't have to work in stone!"

Three weeks later I showed up in that little town for sculptors, Pietrasanta. Little did I know that my life would never be the same.

The morning after I arrived in Italy, I practically floated across the narrow cobblestone street to the studio where I would take my clay class. I turned the squeaky metal handle, pushed open the heavy wooden doors and the noise hit me like a ton of bricks. Goggled carvers, buzzing tools in hand, were busy air-hammering and chiseling away at their pieces. Marble chips flew in all directions, and stone dust covered every inch of the place. Surrounded by life-size plaster models—saints, madonnas, cherubs and draped figures—I was in awe, and a bit irritated. What happened to "playing in clay?"

"You're going to carve in marble like everyone else!" Bernice announced. *What?* How could I, someone who had never gotten dirty, never worn jeans, never gone without makeup, never used power tools—or, for that matter, *any* tools—carve in one of the most sought-after, hardest materials to tackle?

"But... but I have no experience, like all of these other people," I protested, holding fast to my belief that I was not "good enough" to be an artist.

Undaunted, Bernice placed her hand on my shoulder and said, "You start here."

I wanted to run, but as I watched the carvers working, creating, I thought, *I might be able to make something beautiful.* I said to myself, *Here you are, in Michelangelo's backyard, the home of Renaissance paintings and beautiful marble sculptures—just go for*

> *I showed up each day. No matter the noise, the mess, the difficulty, the blinding dust, despite my fear of looking foolish, I just kept showing up. I declared: I am willing to be a beginner.*

it. Give it a shot. What's the worst that could happen? It was the voice of my heart, whispering my deepest desires. It was the voice of the young girl who fell in love with art. It was the voice of the artist I would soon become, urging me to step into my own.

From that moment on, despite my lack of skills and my trepidation, despite the fact that I felt awkward and uncomfortable, despite the fact that this was not my idea of creating art, I was determined to carve something beautiful. I showed up each day. No matter the noise, the mess, the difficulty, the blinding dust, despite my fear of looking foolish, I just kept showing up. I declared: *I am willing to be a beginner.*

After a few clumsy and frustrating weeks, I was able to complete a very simple, Picasso-esque torso with the help of my teacher and the *artigiani* (artisans). But I still didn't know what I was doing, not really, and the joy of "creating art" eluded me. But I kept showing up. I kept practicing. I kept learning. I loved the charming town, with its many twelfth-century buildings, its carved wooden doors, bronze doorknockers and green-shuttered windows. I enjoyed so many new things: the art galleries; little shops; fabulous restaurants; and the countryside around Pietrasanta, with its exquisite green hills, marble mountains and white beaches.

Then one day, it happened: I got inspired. A beautiful, red-haired model walked into our drawing class to pose. She possessed the voluptuous hips, full breasts and heart-shaped tush that, to

> *Only later was it clear to me that I had been sculpting myself.*

me, exemplified a woman. As if in a trance, I began to sketch, and later photographed her in the same pose. The next day, with great anticipation, I brought my pictures to the carving class. I found a stunning piece of pink Portuguese marble—perfect for the piece. I thought, *Now I have something I want to create!*

As I worked I realized I was no longer afraid, nor worried that my work would be good enough. For the first time I thought, *this is fun!* I became more and more excited as I used a point tool to release the figure from its stone cocoon, a toothed chisel for her long flowing hair, a flat chisel to smooth her body, and brought my creation to life. It was challenging, messy and unfamiliar—and still frightening to think I might ruin my creation with one misplaced blow from the hammer—but *it was fun.* As the girl emerged from the marble, I was emerging from my own cocoon, and becoming an artist. Only later was it clear to me that I had been sculpting myself.

One late spring afternoon, about five years after my first trip to Pietrasanta (I'd been back a few times since), I caught a glimpse of the art in my living room. I paused to gaze at the marble carvings and the goddess paintings on my living room walls. I edged closer, and then stopped as if transfixed. Spellbound, I literally could not move. It was the first time I had stopped to take it all in, to really see what was in front of me and all around me—beautiful shapes, forms and colors, all created by me! I could not believe my eyes.

Oh my God. I AM an artist. The words kept repeating in my head, until suddenly I was repeating them out loud. I had worked for years improving my craft, learning to paint and experimenting in a variety of media, maintaining my therapy practice all the while. But I hadn't considered myself a true artist—until now. Heart pounding, it dawned on me that that the dream I had denied myself so many years before had come true. Tears welled up in my eyes and rolled down my cheeks. *I am living a life I love. I am sculpting a beautiful life!*

I've come to realize that if you're drawn to something, if it fills you with joy when you think about it or do it, you *must* pay attention. Follow your long-held dreams, even if you have fears or doubts. Honor what makes you feel alive. Don't ignore it. *Become yourself.* You, too, can live a life you love. My wish for you is that you will sculpt your own beautiful life—now. Just begin.

Alisa Gabrielle (Alisa Blatt, MA, MFT) is an award-winning, multi-faceted artist who draws on her thirty years as a licensed Marriage and Family Therapist, teacher, speaker and workshop leader to help people "sculpt a life they love." Founder and former Director of The California Psychotherapy and Counseling Center, Alisa combines her two professions— artist and therapist/coach to help others follow their heart and live the life of their dreams. She has been a guest on local TV and radio shows, and speaks to organizations and schools. Alisa's art honors women and humanity. Her paintings and sculptures are exhibited and collected internationally, and have been featured on television and in magazines and newspapers. She teaches sculpting and painting classes in Arizona, California and Italy, and offers "Nurturing Your Inner Artist" retreats at her Sedona studio. She is currently writing a memoir about her artistic awakening in Italy, Sculpting a Beautiful Life. *Connect with Alisa at www.AlisaGabrielle.com.*

Pauline Victoria

THE TEACHING DARKNESS

As children, we learn to fear the darkness. We may need a story before bed, and the nightlight on, to distract us from the uncomfortable unknown of the dark. As adults, we are not so easily soothed. It becomes about the dark side of life experience, and emotion. Because we don't want to feel hurt, sorrow or disappointment, we fear the tough times in our lives. Not seeing the richness and possibility the dark contains, we tend to try to speed through it. But I'm here to tell you: the tough times are when your story gets good. Without the darkness, how would you know your light? How would you know the amazing things you are capable of?

Achieving any dream, big or small, is a victory. My dream was always a simple one—to have a full life. For someone without arms and legs, that's a *big* one. And yet, I've got it. A happy marriage; a healthy, treasured son; my own home; a career and a measure of independence I didn't know I could possess—all these are aspects of life I enjoy that some born with all their limbs might not feel able to reach. My life was won through my determination not only to get through the tough times, but to learn from them. They've shown me what I'm here for, what I'm meant to teach. I'm here to encourage and empower people to take up life's reins, rather than play it safe. And if I can do it, I promise you that anyone can.

Unlike most births, met with pure joy and anticipation, mine was a shocking and solemn event. I was born on August 10, 1975, at Travis Air Force Base in California, to an immigrant Filipino woman and a farm-raised Minnesotan man. The doctors delivered the unexpected news of my condition to my father, who revealed to my mother that their first child had been born without arms and legs. She responded by uttering four words: "Thy will be done." My

> But I'm here to tell you: the tough times are when your story gets good. Without the darkness, how would you know your light? How would you know the amazing things you are capable of?

parents approached this unforeseen circumstance with acceptance, faith in God and a practical attitude. Rather than institutionalize me, as was recommended, they chose to embrace me for who I was. That single choice set the tone for my life. When others say, "You can't," I always say, "I *can*."

I always felt loved, accepted, included, nurtured and encouraged. If I wanted to fly across the water on an inner tube behind a boat, we'd make it happen. My parents advocated for me in school, using every available resource and making sure I had equal access. Raised with high standards of achievement, I excelled in school academically and, for the most part, I acclimated socially, too.

As a little girl, I began to notice that others seemed to be deeply affected by me. I didn't do anything special; I was just being a happy little girl, playing with my younger sister. But somehow, seeing me, people were moved. Complete strangers confided in me. They saw my circumstances and my happy nature and felt inspired. So, from an early age, I knew I had this sweet gift, this ability to touch others' hearts.

Life in junior high and high school was tougher. It's a sensitive time for *any* kid. And, as I yearned for the kind of independence my friends had—going out whenever they felt like it, driving, dating—I often felt isolated and frustrated that I didn't get to have the normal experiences other kids take for granted. Sometimes I would cry, I would yell. And then a sense of calm would wash over me. I felt something, some inner voice saying, "It's okay. Your suffering is not in vain. There is a bigger purpose here." In my suffering came my surrender. And I learned a different kind of independence, founded on something bigger than me. Through my faith, I learned to embrace my individuality and become less fearful of being alone. I had to go through the darkness to see the light, to see that it was up to me to make my life whole.

I became very determined to strike out on my own and attend college. It was a big leap of faith, leaving the security of my family home. I was entering a world of strangers who wouldn't understand my needs. How would I ask for help? I'd have to make myself

> *I had to go through the darkness to see the light, to see that it was up to me to make my life whole.*

vulnerable in so many ways. But something inside me said, "You need to go in order to grow." And, as the time came to leave my home and live in the dorms at Santa Clara University, I didn't worry too much. I just went, trusting in the natural human condition to be compassionate and loving, and figured everything would show up as needed. My family was nearby, which was a great comfort to all of us as I struck off into the unknown.

When I have that trust in God, that I'm following what He wants, I guess I just don't struggle with doubt. And my trust was rewarded with a full experience. I had a fabulous roommate, who not only lived in the dorm with me for the first two years of college, but also moved into an apartment with me for the last two. It was a little scary to ask her, "Hey, if I'm in the bathroom and need help, could you come and get me?" She was so nonchalant about it, so easy to be with, that I thought she had previous experience with disabled people. She didn't—she was simply a blessing, a great friend and the right person at the right time. As I pursue my dreams, these people just keep showing up.

After graduation, I settled on working within the corporate world, knowing I would keep pursuing my vision of reaching others and positively changing the world. During that time, I began dating Ted, who was a single dad raising his children from a previous marriage. In 2002, when we married, we became an instant family. Life was a dream. I had bought my first house at the age of twenty-three, got married and was raising children! Life had opened up to an extent that I hadn't thought possible, back in my days of isolation.

Plenty of obstacles came my way, and still do. The obvious ones exist in the physical world; I can go to the beach, for instance, but I'm not free to jump into the waves. Some buildings remain inaccessible to me. Most processes that others take for granted entail a lot of consideration and planning for me.

Other obstacles are social. Out in the world, I get a lot of peculiar looks from people (along with plenty of openness and appreciative feedback). People sometimes don't believe I'm capable of what I do, and can come off as very judgmental. Oftentimes, curious kids approach to ask me questions. "What *happened* to you?" they ask. That's fine with me—it's great, actually. What *is* hard to see is the reactions of their parents. I've seen kids being spanked for talking to me, for being "rude." Most often, they're shushed. So, sadly, they learn to avert their eyes from whom and what is different and mysterious in the world. Obstacles have real teaching power.

The state of California took seven years to grant me a driver's license. Through the process, I sometimes felt discouraged, but I learned to insist that if there was *any* inkling that I could accomplish what I wished to do, I must do it—and I must be allowed to try. Others' unwillingness to believe in my capabilities made me all the more determined. I finally got my driver's license and an adaptive van, which I can drive independently.

When I became pregnant, my husband and I were overjoyed. With the pregnancy, however, a new set of challenges arose. Without limbs, I rely on the bending and flexibility of my torso to accomplish much of what I do. My van was specifically built for my non-pregnant body. A big belly inhibited my ability to get around, drive and perform basic tasks. My husband, Ted, was laid off at around this time, in the post-9/11 economic crash. But this, too, turned out to be a blessing and an opportunity.

Because my husband wasn't working, he was able to be there for me 24/7, driving me to work and helping me with absolutely everything. I had such wonderful support from him, and from a hypno-birthing therapist who worked in our home (an advantage of being disabled!) to guide me into a calm perspective toward labor and delivery. This process can be scary for any woman, and

> *It's through our suffering that we find the opportunity to grow. The happy times of celebration are great, but they're not where the juiciness really lies. The story really gets good when you climb that mountain.*

presents unique challenges for a woman like me. But with their help, I accepted my pregnancy and impending labor as part of a natural, joyful process. I faced the darkness of the unknown with faith, and in April 2006 gave birth to my healthy, beautiful son.

Now that my son is in preschool, I am beginning another life chapter. As I enter into this unknown arena of speaking and writing to make a positive difference on a massive scale, I enter into the dark with only faith and great expectation. My life is my message, and how I choose to live it—in love, joy and possibility.

In safety there is security, predictability. But it's also boring, and rife with regret. Who wants to live in "what if?" Not me. If I had played it safe, I'd still be living at my mother's house. (I certainly love her, but I wouldn't feel fulfilled living that way.) If I hadn't gone to college, I'd have no idea what I was capable of as an independent person. Maybe I wouldn't have gotten married or had a child. And that would have meant I was just settling. There's no reason to settle for less than your dreams. You just have to go through the darkness in order to reach your light. It gives your life purpose, and shows you what you're made of. It's through our suffering that we find the opportunity to grow. The happy times of celebration are great, but they're not where the juiciness really lies. The story *really* gets good when you climb that mountain.

My name, Pauline Victoria, means "small victories." The full life I describe here is made up of a series of those. I can look back on it with great dignity, because I accepted the darkness as I walked the unpaved path toward a life of light. My story may be unusual in some ways, but I don't consider myself special, or more capable than anyone else; rather, I see that my experience can teach others to celebrate their own small victories. In them, one can truly find greatness. In my experience, when I surrender myself to what the dark has to teach, God often gives me more than I could ever dream. He already has.

Born without arms and legs to a loving, supportive family, Pauline Victoria has never let her physical challenges, or being different, get in the way of her pursuit of a fulfilling life. Independently attending college, she subsequently worked in the corporate world and as Disability Program Navigator for the city of Sunnyvale, California, making structural differences in the way people with disabilities access employment resources and helping companies to embrace the strengths and diversities disabled people bring to the workforce. She married Ted in 2002 and gave birth to their son in 2006. She and her family now live on the Big Island of Hawaii.

Simply by being herself, Pauline has had an inspiring, positive impact on those around her since she was a little girl. Today, her mission to reach and uplift larger numbers of people through writing and public speaking has added another dimension of fulfillment and joy to her extraordinary life. Learn more about Pauline at www.PaulineVictoria.com.

Akua Boyenne, Esq.

NO FEAR, NO FEAR, NO FEAR

It was another typical eighty-degree day in Southern California. Navigating through Los Angeles traffic, I watched the sunset descend over the horizon as soothing tones of jazz music escaped my convertible. My cell phone rang. A woman's stoic, unfamiliar voice asked, "Are you Akua?" "Yes, who's calling?" I responded.

"He's been asking for you... calling your name. We finally found your name in his cell phone," the woman explained. Startled, I asked, "Who's been asking for me?" Worried, my mind began to race. *Who could it be? What happened? A client? A friend? Someone in my family...* "Is Dr. William B. Jones your father?" she inquired in a monotonous voice.

I felt as if I had been transported onto a tightrope ten-thousand feet above the ground, with no safety net below me. Frightened and confused, but still composed, I answered, "Yes." The woman said, "He's at UCLA Hospital." Waves of denial rising over me, I caught my breath. "My dad is retired now, he doesn't work at UCLA," I informed her. "I know," she replied. "He's a patient here in the emergency room. He's been in a very serious accident... how quickly can you get here?"

Denial instantaneously transformed into grief and despair. Like James Stewart in the Hitchcock film *Vertigo,* my world began to spin and I could not get my bearing. My father, my best friend, my *hero,* had been paralyzed in a car accident while driving to one of his favorite activities: hitting golf balls at the driving range. Suddenly that California picture-perfect sunny day felt as cold as a New York blizzard. The tightrope snapped. My world as I knew it began to collapse. I was tumbling, reaching out for something to hold on to, only to be left grasping a handful of air. In the blink of an eye I descended into the abyss of a waking nightmare... I was lost.

One week later, as I sat in the UCLA Intensive Care Unit (ICU), one of the doctors attending my father gave me the prognosis. "He will have to remain on a respirator, and he'll no longer be able to

> *I felt like I had been transported onto a tightrope ten-thousand feet above the ground, with no safety net below me.*

move from his neck down." Stunned speechless, I couldn't help but reflect on the irony of it all. This pillar of a man, who had dedicated his life to healing others, was facing the real possibility of not being healed himself.

I reflected on the beautiful, charmed childhood my parents gave me. Having come from an impoverished childhood, my father was committed to providing his children with the best of everything. Being the youngest of three and the only girl, I was showered with love and attention. I often joked that our real family life closely paralleled the Huxtables' TV life, and the creators of *The Cosby Show* owed our family residuals. Like Bill Cosby's fictional character Cliff Huxtable, my father was not only a truly great dad but also a highly respected and well-loved community doctor.

As a child, my identity was greatly influenced by my father. For years, people referred to me as "Dr. Jones's daughter." As I grew older, I came to understand that my father's stature had given me instant recognition and social standing just by mere association. My identity was rooted in my father's reputation and accomplishments. And to a great extent, my peers and I judged our self-worth by titles, material wealth and acquisition.

My parents were the architects of my values, and those family values were reinforced by my environment. Despite flirtations with "bad boys," when it came time to settle down and choose a husband, those values kicked in. I, like my mother and grandmother before her, married a well-known and respected physician. I continued to enjoy the pleasures of a charmed life. I worked as an entertainment attorney for a Beverly Hills law firm, lived in Marina Del Rey, drove a convertible Jaguar and then, rather than being known as "the doctor's daughter," I strongly identified with and became "the doctor's wife."

Now, sitting at my father's bedside, I felt little attachment to the status and the trappings of life. My only thoughts were with him, my only prayers *for* him. I watched as my father painstakingly communicated with the doctors (his peers) about the severity of his injuries and the stark reality of his condition. I held my composure and reminded him that "doctors make mistakes" and "we could prove them wrong." For three weeks I practically lived in the ICU, and spent hours observing physical therapists so I could learn the exercises to heal my father.

One very late night at the end of the third week, my father began reflecting on his life, his commitment to his children and his deepest desire for us to live a happy life. With tears in his eyes, he said, "The intention behind all of my thoughts and actions, as a father, was to provide all of you with the knowledge and tools to make educated and powerful choices." As I held his hand, he made me promise to take care of my mother and to live a fulfilled life. I nodded, unable to speak. *I promise, Dad.*

A few moments later he gently said, "Don't be afraid to live... what do you really want?" In that moment I realized I could not articulate my deep desires, my sincere hopes, my true dreams. *What is really important to me?* The simple question seemed so overwhelmingly complex to me. I had been so rooted in the external world—my father's question made it painfully apparent that I had never really taken the time to ask myself the fundamental questions. *What do I really want in life? What are my dreams?*

Having made the decision not to live his life dependent on a respirator, my father summoned our immediate family to his hospital room the following day. With all of us standing at his bedside, the nurse began shutting down each machine. As the beeps and hums and other sounds stopped and the room became

> *It dawned on me for the first time that, as a result of not knowing myself, I was missing out on contributing my gifts to the world.*

silent, my father looked me in the eyes, and with a murmur that transcended thought and resonated in the core of my being, he whispered his final gift to me as he passed away: "No fear... no fear... no fear..."

Several months after my father passed, I was still trying to make sense of his dying. I kept hearing his last words: *No fear. No fear. No fear.*

I began steeping myself in spiritual writings by Thomas Troward, Ernest Holmes, Joel Goldsmith, Michael Beckwith and Ralph Waldo Emerson. I came across a passage written by Emerson that touched my soul deeply. Emerson wrote, "The death of a dear friend, wife, brother, lover [father], which seemed nothing but privation, somewhat later assumes the aspect of a guide or genius; for it commonly operates revolutions in our way of life, terminates an epoch of infancy or of youth which was waiting to be closed, *breaks up a wonted occupation,* or a household, *or style of living,* and allows the formation of new ones more friendly to the growth of character."

It dawned on me for the first time that, as a result of not knowing myself, I was missing out on contributing my gifts to the world. I knew there was more to me that had yet to be discovered, more of me that I wanted to express. I had been so preoccupied with measuring up to superficial societal expectations that I had not realized how I had been conditioned to surrender my authentic identity and expression.

As an attorney, I had been trained to use my logic, and therefore ignored any guidance from within. Outward appearances would have one believe my dreams had already come true, but inwardly there was a nagging feeling that something was missing. And now, with my hero gone and his parting words echoing in my mind, I could no longer find refuge outside of myself. For the first time, I was forced to go deeper within and ask, "What makes me happy, *really?* What is my soul's purpose? What *are* my dreams?" I listened closer to that small, knowing voice and it began to guide my life in a new direction.

Before my father spoke his last words, my law practice was primarily based on status and prestige. My marriage was based on status and prestige. My social life was based on status and prestige. As a result of being honest with myself, it became crystal clear that

> *When you allow your authenticity to shine through, you share your gifts and knowledge effortlessly.*

if I was going to have a meaningful life, I would have to release people, places and ideas that no longer served me. The gap between knowing what I should do and accessing the courage to actually do it seemed unfathomable.

Familiar with my life as I knew it, I was afraid to move on. I was afraid of the unknown, and somehow believed the unknown would be more emotionally painful than life as I knew it. Releasing my old, comfortable, prestigious life seemed like being dropped into an emotional hurricane in the middle of an ocean—I clung to my father's last words like a life vest. *No fear. No fear. No fear.*

Drawing courage from his memory, I chose to honor my father by living a life based on spiritual principles. Exactly one year after his passing, I opened my own firm and shifted my whole perspective of running a business and practicing law, adding an empowerment and educational component to my practice. To some it may have seemed crazy—a law firm negotiating contracts based on spiritual principles? But to me, it was the dream I never knew I had until my father's death, as Emerson wrote, brought on a "revolution" in my way of life and forced me to listen to the still, small voice within. My father had given me love and many material things, but his final gift to me would be a gift I could draw on for the rest of my life.

Inspired by my own search for meaning, my own drive to live an authentic life, I dedicated my practice to encouraging clients to gain clarity about their options and articulate what is *really* important to them, and then negotiating powerfully on their behalf to achieve not just their goals, but their heart's desires.

When you allow your authenticity to shine through, you share your gifts and knowledge effortlessly. You know you are finally living your dreams because it feels wonderful just to be *you!*

Akua Boyenne, Esq. is a Los Angeles-based entertainment attorney specializing in motion picture and television transactions. Her clients include award-winning and aspiring writers, directors, actors, producers and production companies that work in both the studio and independent systems. Akua is a graduate of Seton Hall Law School, Tufts University and extensive programs at UCLA Entertainment Law Studies. She is admitted to practice in California, New York and New Jersey, and is a member of the American Bar Association (Entertainment Law Section), the Beverly Hills Bar Association (Entertainment and Intellectual Property Section), Film Independent, Inc. and Women in Film, Inc. She frequently speaks to large groups at colleges, spiritual centers, film festivals and other entertainment events. Connect with Akua at www.BoyenneLaw.com.

John L. Edwards

MAKE A DIFFERENCE

I told the teenage boy, Chaba, sitting before me, "I've got something for you." I produced a pair of brand new boots. Chaba's face lit up, then twisted in confusion. I looked down at his bare, calloused feet covered with sores, blisters and scars inflicted by the gravel and broken bottles of the streets he walked daily. I prepared a basin of warm disinfected water and set it down in front of him. He looked up at me fearfully, then took a deep breath and lowered his feet into the water. His body twitched and he hissed between clenched teeth, pulling his feet back from the water. He shook his head.

I knelt down and took his swollen feet in my hands and began to gently wash them in the basin. Chaba's tear-streaked face continued to quiver with each touch, but he never took his eyes off me, the disbelief radiating like a coal oven, yet newly stoked with hope. I felt it in myself; the disbelief, the out-of-body serenity. What was I doing here, on my knees, washing the feet of this young thief and murderer?

I smiled. "Are these truly the face and feet of a top-notch killer? Why would you want to cause others so much pain when you can't even handle the pain of washing your own feet?" He pulled his feet from the basin, quickly dried them with a towel. Then, without a word, he grabbed his boots and left the room. I looked back down into the basin of water, brown with dirt and flesh. I let it pull me down into the painful past, into my own memories of growing up in Jamaica.

I was a bad kid. There was no other way to explain it. I was born bad. A fighter. A vandal. No purpose in life. Always in trouble. I was a wanted kid, and not in the good sense. Everybody had a grudge against me, even my family. My mother was a teacher; my father did what he could to make ends meet, as well as he could. But

> *I looked back down into the basin of water, brown with dirt and flesh. I let it pull me down into the painful past, into my own memories of growing up in Jamaica.*

no running water. No car. No electricity. Our village of unpaved roads was riddled with poverty and crime. I didn't realize it then, but my environment was already shaping my future.

Education finally put me on the right track, that and the self-sacrifice and helping hands of my family and friends. My mother saw the potential in me. I had a natural affinity for learning. My mother made it clear that my studies were the priority; and once I realized this, everything changed. It got me off the streets, focused my life; it taught me self-discipline and self-worth. And at every step, my family continued to sacrifice for my betterment. I was the first in the family accepted into college. There was no money for the basic necessities, but when it came time to go my father sold forty acres of land that he owned, at pennies on the dollar, and gave it to me for room and board and books. These lessons would stay with me and inform everything I did in the future.

After graduation from college I started working in a brewing and bottling factory on the outskirts of an incredibly impoverished Garrison near the city of Kingston, a dangerous underworld where I met the children who would change my life. You needed an "escort" to gain entry, and here I met the people who allowed me that entry, and it changed my life. I met boys like Chaba, street urchins, killers and thieves with no family, no hope, no dreams. They were too busy finding a way to fulfill the basic necessities of life to even think about dreaming.

Children who don't dream? What I saw was so painful I would return home at night and cry myself to sleep. I began to write down my experiences. I had never written before, but this was my only emotional outlet, the only way to express myself and to remember what needed to be remembered. I was inspired to bring the stories of this impoverished area to the big screen. It became a dream of mine to create a film, to draw attention to these forgotten children. I studied screenwriting and began the long task of putting together a screenplay.

I worked hard, building my dreams on three simple pillars: faith, wisdom and the near-compulsive willingness to take a risk. My spiritual faith gave me a razor-sharp focus; my education, life

> *I immersed myself in the struggle for material and monetary wealth, and for a time I forgot about those boys I had lived with for almost three years. Most of them were dead by the time I left for the United States.*

experience and mentorship gave me wisdom. And I constantly leveraged my limited resources to invest in value propositions I thoroughly understood. Another opportunity appeared in my life and suddenly I went from my work at the factory to a highly lucrative career on Wall Street in the United States. I immersed myself in the struggle for material and monetary wealth, and for a time I forgot about those boys I had lived with for almost three years. Most of them were dead by the time I left for the United States.

In 1995, my life changed. Within two months, both of my older brothers died. The deaths were completely unrelated, but the cumulative effect hit me like a thunderbolt. *How could God take my two wealthiest and most attractive brothers and yet leave me here?*

It led me to ponder why we place so much emphasis on material wealth and physical beauty. My system of values was so shocked and my discouragement so deep that I soon quit my job on Wall Street and turned inward. The things I had believed in now seemed meaningless, and I shifted into a time of dark emotions and deep contemplation.

I realized that the dreams that mattered weren't about material gain; they were the dreams about change, what I did for others, the social good that came as a direct result of my actions. Encouraged by my family and friends and inspired by my faith, I returned to the working world as an educator for urban communities, seeking

> *I realized that the dreams that mattered weren't about material gain; they were the dreams about change, what I did for others, the social good that came as a direct result of my actions.*

to inspire and give back rather than merely accumulate wealth and material goods for myself.

The story of those children in the Garrison resurfaced and stayed with me, and the dream of making a film remained with me, too. Yet with all my classes on screenwriting and research on filmmaking, the script remained unfinished eight years in. The art of the screenplay seemed clearly beyond me. I was still an analyst, not an author, but I refused to give up. There had to be another way.

I returned to the beginning, to the stories themselves. I began re-imagining the boys, and myself, as fictional characters, and something clicked. The floodgates opened and the writing flowed. I completed the novel, *Price of Humans,* in eight months! Now I had something tangible. Source material. I could envision commercial success in print first, then the film. The feeling of completion was indescribable.

The memories flooded back. I remembered one day in court. Chaba had been arrested for murder and they had brought him into the courtroom, his shirt and pants dirty and tattered, displayed like the "trash" they thought he was. Unbeknownst to him, my lawyer and I sat in the back. The judge, with his imperious gaze directed at Chaba, proclaimed to him, "Since you have no lawyer, you will not be entitled to bail."

I nudged the lawyer and he cried out, "Your honor, I'm representing the defendant!" All eyes turned to us. Chaba smiled.

The judge reluctantly changed his ruling and allowed bail. "Your client still poses a serious threat so I am setting the bail at half a million dollars!" Everyone in the courtroom gasped. Chaba flinched as if he'd been shocked with electricity. The lawyer sighed. The judge grinned and continued, "Since it's unlikely that you will be able to post this bail, I hereby…" He assigned Chaba to a maximum security facility.

"Your honor, we will accept these conditions and post bail for the defendant," I snapped back. Everyone stared at us. Who would pay such a price to help someone who seemed so insignificant? Who indeed? I was simply a man, living his life. Today, I am simply a man with a story to tell. The story of Chaba and countless other young men who live in the Garrison. Boys who, like Chaba, will die too soon. Boys who cannot dream bigger than a clean bed, a full plate and a safe place to sleep. Boys who would give anything to live the life you are living right now.

And my message is this: If you are already living the life of someone else's dreams, what's stopping you from going after your own? Fight for your dreams as passionately as the boys in the Garrison fought for food, for a pair of shoes, for their lives. And carry the spirit of the less fortunate—those who have touched YOUR life—carry that spirit with you as you doggedly pursue your own dreams. I know I will always carry the Garrison boys with me as I fight for mine. So take the risk. Make it count. Make a difference.

Jamaican born John L. Edwards, BsSc., DMS, EMBA, is an educator, author, youth-advocate and stocks/options investment guru. Plans are underway to turn into a film his first novel, Price of Humans, *based on his experiences in the ghettos of Kingston. John started his career brewing/bottling internationally known brands of beers and beverages and later moved to Wall Street. He now works as a school administrator and spends a great deal of time training educators and exploring his passion for writing. In the early 1990s John created his first International Youth Camp at The University of The West Indies and Paisley Gardens, Portland, Jamaica, an academic and cultural melting ground for inner-city college and high school students.*

Working closely with CEOs of large firms and Fortune 500 companies, John continues to teach groups of people how to invest and manage their investment portfolios. His philanthropic efforts are mostly channeled through his non-profit organization (FEDERAN) whose mission focuses on youth, education and community development. Connect with John at www.PriceOfHumans.com.

Nadine Lajoie

THE RACE OF YOUR LIFE

Racing: It's all about freedom, adrenalin and speed. It's about your hair whipping in the wind, the world blurring past, and being so in the moment of what you're doing that even though everything is fast, it seems like slow motion. It's about never losing sight of the finish line, but concentrating on what you need to do next—weave to the right, ease to the left, prepare to maneuver the next corner. It's about acquiring new tools and tricks and using them. It's about so much, but most of all, it's about having fun. It's about all of these things, whatever the race may be—a foot race, a horse race, a motorcycle race, or the race of your days on the road of life.

I never intended to race motorcycles. That's not to say I didn't dream of riding them. I fell in love with motorcycles when I was just a child. At sixteen I made my dad buy a motorcycle for both of us, but after I had a minor accident, Dad forbade me to ride it.

Before that, I played volleyball competitively. My dream was to reach the Canadian championships, which I did in 2000 (we finished ninth in beach volley 2x2, though I'm only five-feet one-inch tall). I broke my knee five times in the preceding four years. The last time, I needed surgery. I could no longer play volleyball at the highest level, so I decided to realize my dream of motorcycling. No matter what the race is, the unexpected does occur: divorce, illness, job loss, someone crashing into you. When the unexpected arises, you don't quit. You greet it as a transforming challenge, and look for solutions.

The first thing I did was buy a new motorcycle. Initially, I was interested in just riding, not racing, and that's what I did for two years—street riding. But eventually I found myself trailing the fastest drivers on the road and touching my pegs in the curves. A friend told me, "You are too crazy and dangerous for the streets. You need to go race." He was right.

> It's about all of these things, whatever the race may be—a foot race, a horse race, a motorcycle race, or the race of your days on the road of life.

Racing is a male-dominated sport, but in 2003, a track in Quebec opened a women's series. I didn't have enough money to buy a racing bike, but for the last race, two of my friends and I pitched in to buy one. I rode that cycle up to the starting line.

It's almost impossible for me to describe the exhilaration of that first race. It was simply awesome. I discovered I had a natural skill for motorcycle racing. And even though I didn't win the race (finishing third), I did win a new outlook on life, an overwhelming sense of optimism and happiness. I also won a new focus, a new ambition, a new direction in which to steer my personal drive.

I became a full-fledged racer, racing against both women and men. During the next few years, I raced seventeen weekends a year, three or four races a weekend. That's a lot, because preparation and traveling required my time from Thursday through Sunday. After a couple of years of this, I set myself a new goal: I wanted to travel alone through the United States and race at different tracks all across the country.

I told my friends what I wanted to do. I said that I would sell my house, sell my car, get an RV and just go. They all said I was crazy, and discouraged me—so throughout my planning process, I pretty much kept my own counsel. It took me ten months to plan the trip. I plotted which cities I would visit, where I would sleep, how I would manage my business from the road. I also created a Dream Book. In it, I wrote down all of my dreams and pasted in many inspiring pictures. I dedicated each page to a different topic, and whenever I thought of a new problem involved in achieving my dream, I wrote it down on the proper page and found a solution.

My trip was awesome! I slept wherever I could—truck stops, shopping center parking lots—and I raced on tracks across the United States. To travel alone, I really had to go outside of my comfort zone. Similarly, in order to race against men, I had to overcome my fear. While I never stop thinking about my ultimate goals, I find that if I focus just on the next thing I need to do, I'm much better able to combat my fears.

> *No matter what the race is, the unexpected does occur: divorce, illness, job loss, someone crashing into you. When the unexpected arises, you don't quit. You greet it as a transforming challenge, and look for solutions.*

In the 2006-2007 racing season, I set the goal of competing in the famous Bike Week races at Daytona. I just wanted to qualify in the top thirty of the approximately seventy-five competitors. On the day of the race, it rained, and I got angry. Not only would rain make racing harder; I, unlike other racers who had personal mechanics, was my own mechanic. I would have to change my tires myself, in the rain.

Then I realized that if I kept my negative attitude, I would never have a good race. So much about good racing, in life or on the track, is about a positive attitude. So I consciously changed my attitude.

First, I told myself that I was actually at an advantage because of the rain. In Canada, it rains a lot, so I was used to racing on wet tracks, while my competitors were not. Then I thought, *I'm blessed to be my own mechanic*. Whenever people along the way gave me tips on how to fix my bike, I took good notes. And because I was so good at learning lessons, I was much more independent.

Then I began to visualize a successful race. My starts were often the worst part of my race, but the week before a fellow racer had given me some great advice on starts. I visualized myself in third

> *You don't need money to succeed, and you don't need to rely on others. You just need your dreams, and to know how to handle the next corner in the race towards your goals.*

or fourth place after the first corner. I also visualized a nice white energy coming onto the track to protect all racers, and I visualized an additional purple bubble of energy on the track for added safety.

The race began, and by the first corner, I was in second place. I'd had some friends who'd died on the tracks over the years, so mentally I had them on the back of my cycle, and we rode together, making the race fun. I didn't concern myself with the finish. I just focused on what I had to do at each corner. In the rain, you really need to be smooth, so I concentrated on dancing with the bike, dancing in the rain.

On the last lap, one guy passed me, and when I finished, I wasn't sure what place I was in because I'd lapped a few other racers. I thought I might have been fifth. I got off my cycle, and people were congratulating me, but it wasn't until I heard my name announced that I realized I'd finished in third place. Third place at Daytona! I was walking on clouds.

That win changed my life. It opened the United States racing market for me. I had interviews in the media. I gained a whole network of people who thought very differently from people I'd met so far, especially in Quebec. Thus, I gained entirely new perspectives on so many elements of racing and life. The Daytona win brought so many new opportunities with it that were perfect for business *and* life. I've always lived my life at 180 mph, taking on as many projects as possible. I tell my clients that it's easier to realize your dreams when you have more going on in your life, because you increase your possibilities.

Many people tend to think that success is something someone else can achieve for them. We all need help at certain points along the way, but for the most part, our success relies solely on us. My first business was a financial company I started from scratch, and in three years I had four-hundred-fifty clients. The latest is a real estate investment business in the United States, started two years ago.

You don't need money to succeed, and you don't need to rely on others. You just need your dreams, and to know how to handle the next corner in the race towards your goals. Life, in fact, is a race, as is almost everything in it. There's a starting line and a finish line. Along the way, you have to move at different speeds. There will be detours, since life never plays out the way you think it will. The key to winning the race of life is to visualize the finish line, focus on the next corner and have fun!

An international motorcycle racer, successful motivational speaker, musician and President of Nadynn International Inc. and Lajoie des Finances, Inc., Nadine Lajoie is a multi-talented woman who excels at communicating her passion for life. Her mission is to inspire women's organizations, business organizations and today's youth to IN-Power themselves so they can realize their dreams. She has received the "Excellence Club of Canada" award for seven years, and the Quebec Women's Business Network 2007 "Established Business of the Year" award, all while working only 133 days per year. Contact Nadine at www.NadineRacing.com.

Angela Alexander

MIRACLES IN ACTION

I'm not an author, speaker, or a writer, I repeatedly told myself. I
*know nothing about the publishing industry, marketing, ISBNs,
or booking speaking engagements. I just need to push those thoughts
out and let reality back in.* That enemy from within was talking to
me; I nursed, rehearsed and owned all those negative thoughts for
months.

During this time my guilty conscience took my sleep, peace
and appetite away. While I walked in disobedience I even became
uncomfortable in my skin.

Writing my testimony was my part of my mission, though I
didn't know it at the time. But there was no getting around my
calling, which was very much outside of my comfort zone. We all
have an assignment, and the only way through it is to do it.

In 1996, my sister Alice passed. It was the closest death I had
experienced. A week before Alice's unexpected death, God allowed
her to write a letter. She folded it and tucked it deep in her wallet
like an emergency twenty-dollar bill. After she passed, the police
held her purse as evidence for the investigation. The following
year was the hardest of my life. Visions of her death hounded me
day and night. When the trial finally ended, my sister's personal
belongings were released to my family. Being nosy, I rummaged
through her purse and found the hidden letter.

Alice's first sentence immediately relieved the grief I had embraced. Her thoughts let me know that her death was between her and God. Her letter gave me the peace I had been praying for. Although painful, that year of grief was necessary for the lessons I learned during my walk in the wilderness. The healing that took place was not only about my recovery; it was also about my preparation. During that time I learned that love never dies. Death is inevitable, but misery is optional.

In 2000, my son Murice was in third grade. He had a math test one day; he finished early and received his A. While he waited for his classmates to complete their tests, he wrote a letter to his father and me. Writing that letter was his assignment. After school he ran

> *Twice, the Holy Spirit had Murice write, "Stay together." So many couples separate and divorce after the death of a child or children.*

in the house and shouted, "Mommy, Mommy, Daddy, I wrote you a letter, I wrote you a letter!" He was so excited. "Where are you going?" I asked. "Nowhere. I just love you." I gave him the biggest hug.

My husband, Surie, and I read his letter aloud. Murice not only expressed that he loved us, he explained why he loved us. He let us know he was happy that we were his parents. In a second letter addressed "Dear Mom," he said, "If I got to choose a mom, I would choose you." At the bottom of all three pages, he wrote, "By-by." Sometimes God will show us things but not reveal their intended purpose until His appointed time. Twice, the Holy Spirit had Murice write, "Stay together." So many couples separate and divorce after the death of a child or children.

The death of *my* children. Several weeks later, on April 1, 2000, while I was in Japan on military duty, Lt. Mevehichi summoned me. I had just arrived in the country and couldn't imagine what I had done wrong. When I entered the room and was introduced to the priest, I knew something had happened and it was no April

Fool's joke. My husband and four children had been involved in a fatal car crash. Our truck fell twenty-five feet off the highway and landed upside-down on top of two other parked vehicles with people inside. Praise God they were all right! But my two eight-year-old sons, Murice and Roger, had died instantly.

On the plane ride home, I thanked God that my whole family wasn't taken away. I thanked God that Murice and Roger weren't suffering or waiting for me to come home only then to pass away. Most people think Japan was the worst place possible for me to be, but I thanked God I was there. God knows me: if I had been home, I would have run somewhere and not heard His voice. In Japan, I had no choice but to be still and know that God is still God.

The Thursday before my sons' double memorial service, I stood in the kitchen and prayed. "Dear God, thank you so much for Murice's good-bye letter. It's truly the reason I can stand here right now. However, I need to know that Roger is also at peace." God placed one word in my spirit—*search*. I said, "Search?" So I began praying some more, because I was searching for more clues. I literally searched my home for over three hours, but didn't find anything that gave me the peace I had prayed for.

Only as God can create it, only as God can orchestrate it: there was an open house at my children's school that evening. My two daughters needed some normalcy, so we went and visited all four classrooms. Two weeks before the crash, Roger's teacher had given her students all kinds of arts and crafts supplies. She gave no specific instructions. She just said, "Do something for open house, your parents are coming." We entered Roger's classroom, and there was his project stapled to the wall—the answer to my prayers.

Roger had cut out the shape of a house with double doors. Centered inside was a description: "I have a big house and a big backyard." Wait a minute: we actually have the smallest backyard on our block. Then I realized that Roger was referring to his heavenly home. To the left of his description, he had pasted a tombstone. On that tombstone, he had written three powerful words: "Dead Men Joy." Below those words he had drawn a picture of himself. To the right of his home description, he had placed another tombstone, on which was written, "Dead Men Jams," and drawn a picture of his brother, Murice, who always used to dance and jam around the house. I almost fell to my knees in that classroom, as I marveled at God's many miracles in action. Murice didn't know about Roger's letter, and vice versa. Both listened to the Holy Spirit and obeyed.

While I was writing my sons' memorial program, God revealed to me that all three letters, including the one from my sister, were written to soothe my soul—but, more importantly, to share. The letters were the foundation of my testimony, and that's when my ministry, Miracles in Action, began.

> *I learned that God is not concerned with your ability, but your availability. When God gives you a vision, He's already made the provisions. God has designed you, and His design defines your destiny.*

I was empowered, yes, but still so filled with doubt. I had so many sleepless nights of feeding myself excuses for why I couldn't write a book. After five long months, I woke up and surrendered. I prayed, "Dear Heavenly Father, I am your willing vessel. Use me as You choose—lead me and I'll follow." I knew that publicly sharing God's amazing testimony verbally and in written form was my personal assignment. I learned that God is not concerned with your ability, but your availability. When God gives you a vision, He's already made the provisions. God has designed you, and His design defines your destiny.

But first I had to replace those negative thoughts with positive ones. I began speaking to myself daily: "I can do all things through Christ Jesus who strengthens me. I am an international, inspirational, successful, dynamic and sought-after author and speaker."

When I started my book, I had to ask my daughter how to save a page on the computer. I wrote for a year and a half without knowing how my words were going to transform into a physical book. I wrote on faith. Everything was still a mystery, but it was such a relief and joy to begin what I was assigned to do. It was confirmation that I was on my right path. My problems with eating and sleeping had dissipated. But I had new problems—the struggle of my assignment.

I had many obstacles and obligations, but I would not allow them to stop me. The chapter about my sister's death took over four months to complete, because when I wrote about it I relived the pain. Any time I even considered quitting, I asked myself, *What if Alice, Murice, or Roger listened, but didn't complete their assignments?* As great as their letters are, most people won't know about them unless I finish my mission.

Don't worry about the details as to how it will all work out. Just move forward and know that it's already all right. Don't have such an iron-tight business plan that there's no room for the Holy Spirit

> *Don't worry about the details as to how it will all work out. Just move forward and know that it's already all right. Don't have such an iron-tight business plan that there's no room for the Holy Spirit to have His way.*

to have His way. If you have a purpose and passion that excites your soul, something you would do for free, how could you not pursue the desires of your heart? For two years, every day, I worked on my book. When *Miracles in Action* was hot off the presses, I saw some grammatical errors. I said to myself, "If I ever write another book, I will do things so much differently." The Holy Spirit was listening; He said, "Do it." Because I know what it feels like to walk in disobedience, I set that book aside and began all over again. This time I hired a professional editor. God gave me such an excellent testimony, I needed to present it with excellence.

Once I surrendered, I discovered I had talents and abilities I didn't know I possessed. People should be able to tell what you're waiting for by what you're working on. In order to have a dream come true, you first must *have* a dream. Many people have dreams, some wake up and achieve them. What are you going to do? If you were already there, where would you be?

Angela Alexander is an inspirational speaker who shares her testimony with audiences worldwide. She is the author of Miracles in Action: Turning Pain into Power and Grief into Peace. *Born and raised in St. Louis, she currently lives in southern California and is retired from the U.S. Air Force Reserve.*

Through her testimony, Angela shares how she transformed, transcended and triumphed in the midst of her storm and received God's blessings. Even after reading this condensed version of Miracles in Action, *you, too, will see that God is working His purpose out, He's in control and miracles are always in action. If your church, conference, retreat or book club would like to see Angela share the glory behind the story of this absolutely fascinating, supernatural testimony from the living God we serve, she's more than excited to come out and share! Connect with Angela at www.MiraclesInAction.com.*

Anna Cuevas

QUESTION AUTHORITY

It was Tuesday, July 13th—my daughter's twenty-fifth birthday—when the email from the Gonzalez family came in. The Gonzalezes, a family of four, were desperate for answers. Their house had been sold at a foreclosure sale. One week prior, the family got an unexpected knock on the door from a real estate agent who advised them that their home no longer belonged to them, but to the bank. Several attorneys had told them it was nearly impossible to get the home back, and they were devastated and bewildered—in shock.

They were in disbelief, you see, because the major bank that they had trusted sold their home right out from under them, even though they were in the middle of a Home Affordable Modification Program process. They had been promised that the sale would be postponed, but when they called to find out what happened, they were told that there was nothing they could do. It was too late—the house was already sold.

The injustice of the Gonzalezes' story lit a fire under me. How could a bank whose word this family had trusted turn its back on them? They are not just a loan number; they are a family! I could feel their pain and disappointment, the feeling of being let down by the bank they trusted to do the right thing. And I knew, at that moment, that I would get their home back. There was no doubt in my mind.

We fought the bank, pushing through six executive levels before I hit a wall. I moved on to the Treasury, the Senate Housing Committee, the Judicial Oversight Committee and every single governmental entity I could think of, and hit a wall with them, too. I went to bed that night feeling really frustrated—but not defeated—and when I woke up, I had a new inspiration. "You're going to write to every single person at this big dog bank until you

> *It was too late—the house was already sold.*

get a response," I told myself. By Friday we had the okay to get the sale rescinded. By Saturday, the modification was delivered to the Gonzalezes via Federal Express.

When I heard their voices cracking with tears of amazement, joy and gratitude that their home really was theirs again, it was a profoundly wonderful feeling, worth more than anything to me. And the passion and determination I felt to help the Gonzalez family brought me back to the first intuition I had that my life's work and responsibility was to help people fight to save their homes—their real American dreams.

A few years ago, when the housing market crashed, my husband lost his real estate and mortgage business. He might have made it if his friend and partner had not embezzled 100K—or maybe not. I had gone from making 90K a month as the top-ranking loan executive ever in the history of my company to resigning in fear of its collapse, to writing a $250 check, after a whole month's work at a new lender, to cover my health insurance payment. That company also went under; so did the two companies I worked for next.

My faith began to falter. "Wow," I thought. "What the heck happened to the dream?" Everything was crumbling around me, but I didn't want to give up. People were telling me, "Shortsell your house and go rent an apartment—everybody else has already given up." I said, "No. I'm *not* going to do that." If anything, I wanted to show my kids that you have to fight for what you believe in, and you have to keep going. Even if I lost everything, if at least they would see that I gave it my all and remember that message; that was the most important thing I could give them as a parent. Still, doing multiple jobs and driving around helping people with their businesses just to keep food on the table, I felt myself sinking.

One day, when I was so tired and frustrated I thought I just couldn't do it anymore, I drove over to a meditation center and sat in the meditation garden. I watched the ocean, contemplated my situation and went within to try to find an answer. Driving back home, I passed through Rancho Santa Fe, a very affluent area full of big mansions, sleek cars, people eating at bistros—and it hit me: "What's the difference," I asked, "between me and them? Why am I struggling, while they are not?"

I realized there *was* no difference. *We were all created in the likeness of God,* I reminded myself. *He gave me the gift of talent; my gift back to Him is using it.* I remembered Luke 12:48: "For of those who much is given, much is required." With this revelation, my perspective instantly changed. I decided to come back to working

> *My faith began to falter. "Wow," I thought. "What the heck happened to the dream?"*

on self-motivation. Essentially, I shifted my mentality from "poor me" to "you've got to *do* something." In a climate of fear, I became certain of two things: I would be guided and taken care of. And I needed to serve others in a big way. Empowering them became my priority and personal mission. When you change the quality of your thoughts, you can change your life. Sometimes you just have to step out of your perceived reality to see that that mountain in front of you is not actually a mountain.

My husband and I had been in the real estate business for such a long time, our advocacy for others began with previous clients coming to us for help. I saw the anguish in their faces—whole families would come in crying, and it was heartbreaking. They had been taken advantage of; not just the first time, when they could have gotten a better loan, but then when they had applied for help from unscrupulous attorneys and people who were from agencies that were supposed to help them, but had no intention of doing so. Now they had no clue what to do. In some cases, their houses had already been sold out from under them.

The injustice of it burned me. It fueled me with a deep passion to rectify the wrongs done to these people. I had enough knowledge and information, and I knew how to network. I figured if I was as aggressive as I had been in trying to *get* loans, when I was in the mortgage business, I could be just as aggressive in getting them *fixed*. So I decided to totally devote myself to advocating for victims of foreclosure.

> *When you change the quality of your thoughts, you can change your life. Sometimes you just have to step out of your perceived reality to see that that mountain in front of you is not actually a mountain.*

That was in 2008. Since then, through my advocacy, thousands of people have been spared from losing their homes, and I give people free advice all day long. I feel pretty great about that, but it has to go even further. Now, my vision is to create the broadest possible platform for the delivery of accurate information to people, so they will be empowered to get their dreams back on their own, or with help. I want to help them take their power back—the power they gave up a long time ago when they let people tell them what was happening, rather than figuring out for themselves what was really going on.

There is a very simple three-point plan you can follow to fight for your dreams: 1. Get empowered with accurate information. 2. Take action based on that information. And 3. Question authority! Questioning authority is pretty much the gist of my job. And we all have to. Consumers believe that when they call a bank, the representative they are talking to is giving them the truth, all the accurate information. But the person you talk to could have been working at a department store last week. You can't expect anyone to go above and beyond—they're just working for a living, and they can't always answer correctly because the foreclosure crisis has left no time for training.

More times than not, I find numerous inaccuracies. But when people are told they're being denied for whatever reason, they take that as *the* final answer. And they start packing their stuff to move out of their houses. People are scared—but if we do nothing, we will get nothing. By the same token, how many times do we allow some authority figure or naysayer to tell us we can't have our dream, whether it's someone close to us who tells us we're not qualified, not pretty or smart enough, don't have enough money, et cetera, and we just accept this as fact?

Consider the source of your information. Maybe it's really not true. Often the authority figure we need to question is our own thought process, the one that tells us to just give up on a dream. Don't accept it—don't accept defeat. In this world of infinite possibilities, it is all there for you, waiting for you to claim it. Just change your mindset and anticipate a positive outcome, even when all evidence points to the contrary.

On Mother's Day, 2009, I was diagnosed with ovarian cancer. It is now in remission, after a real miracle. I tell people that if God can work the miracle of putting me in remission from cancer, a little loan modification is no big deal—if you believe. The mind is so strong, and we use only ten percent of it, if that! Imagine what would happen if we engaged it fully and became present in our own lives.

When you look at something as being insurmountable, it becomes insurmountable. So whenever you feel that something is impossible, seek out true stories of people who have survived or accomplished something even bigger than what you are dealing with. Take a deep breath, get into nature, quiet your mind and regroup. Shift your mindset for just a moment. In the moments of our greatest trials we take the biggest leaps in personal growth—IF we change our perspective, extract the lessons of the experience and use all of it to come back stronger and better than ever. Even when a dream seems lost forever—like a home that's already been foreclosed upon and re-sold—it can be won back with belief and perseverance. I've seen it happen again and again.

With all of us staying positive, working hard and believing we would triumph, sure enough—we won the Gonzalez house back. *After the investor had already taken it.* I fought for the Gonzalezes' home with the very essence of my being. That is what you need to do for yourself, for your own dream. No matter who tells you otherwise, believe: you *will* come through.

Anna Cuevas went from being a teenage mother on welfare to being the number one account executive in the United States for a Fortune 500 corporation; from wealth to job loss during the financial crisis; and from a diagnosis of ovarian cancer to remission. Using these opportunities to redefine herself and help others, Anna committed to empowering, and advocating for, consumers. Since 2008, the Cuevas family has facilitated the return of fourteen homes already lost to foreclosure, and helped thousands of people save their homes. An author who has appeared on various web shows, Anna is currently writing a book on spirituality titled Oh My God. *Her book* Save Your Home! Without Losing Your Mind or Your Money *will be released in 2011. Connect with Anna at www.AskALoanModGuru.com, www.TheLoanModGuru.com and www.TheHuffingtonPost.com/Anna-Cuevas.*

Reginald Alfonzo Sizemore

THE LONGEST PROMISE

From two refurbished appliances in the basement, to the garage, to the store on the avenue, to a new addition, to this warehouse, I've come a long way on my journey. When I look at the appliances stacked up to the ceiling, see my employees running around, hear the phone ringing, watch customers streaming in and out—it just makes me smile. And it reminds me of every step I took to get here, to fulfill my father's dreams. I feel him here with me and within me now, seeing proudly through my eyes. And oftentimes, I wonder where I would be if I had not had such a father.

My father, John Perry Sizemore, felt that he had made mistakes in his life. He had married too young, had eight children and never had the chance to live his dreams. But I loved and admired him with all my heart. At a very young age, when he asked me to shine a pair of his shoes, I shined them all. When he asked me to wash the car, I washed the car and the van, and waxed them. I waited to hear him say, "That's my son," or, "I'm proud of you." When I was twelve, I heard him say to his sister, "This guy here, I guarantee he is going to be somebody. This is the only child I have that I don't worry about. Reggie."

I often helped my father with electrical work. One day, he called me over to where he was testing some wires. He asked me to touch two wires. I thought they were "hot." Dad kept on telling me, "Trust me, son, the wires are not hot." I kept saying, "No, no, no!" I finally gave in and touched both wires, not knowing what was going to happen. The wires were dead. Nothing happened. My father said to me, "You are my son, and I will never do anything to hurt you. You can't imagine how good you made me feel by trusting me. I love you. We can trust each other."

When I was about fifteen, my uncle Joseph asked me over to his house: he had something he wanted me to hear. He put on a record, "The Strangest Secret in the World," by Earl Nightingale. As I heard that recording, my whole life lit up. Unbeknownst to me, I had been thinking that same way all along. So I became convinced that my thinking was on the right track. I asked my uncle if I could borrow the album, and I took it home and listened to it every day. When it came time to return it, I just couldn't. I found a phone number leading to Mr. Nightingale on the back of the record and ordered more materials.

Earl Nightingale put into words everything I had been feeling was the right way for me to live: be consistent; believe in yourself; never give up; and understand that everybody is different. He

> *I feel him here with me and within me now, seeing proudly through my eyes. And oftentimes, I wonder where I would be if I had not had such a father.*

taught me that no one is superior, and no one is inferior. You're simply yourself. We're all as different as fingerprints, snowflakes, our signatures, and we do our best. If you do certain things a certain way each day, it will all work out.

After I heard "The Strangest Secret in the World," I went to the mirror and said to myself: *From this point in my life, I'm going to do everything I know and think is right.* Things have been going great ever since. Perhaps because of this commitment, perhaps because of our special relationship or maybe because I had just dropped out of school, my father called me to him one day when

I was sixteen and asked me if I would live his dreams for him. My reply was, immediately, "Yes," though what had to be done was still unknown.

Dad listed the four dreams to be accomplished: Learn to play the guitar; work at the Illuminating Company; graduate from the West Side Institute of Technology and open an appliance store. My desire to please him and to make his dreams a reality became my strength of purpose. Because I would have to graduate from high school to fulfill his dream of attending the West Side Institute, I went back to school and studied day and night, getting straight A's. I graduated, as he had never done. He was so proud of me that he lent me his car for the first time on graduation night. My promise to my father meant more to me than anything else because its fulfillment would please him and make him proud.

His dream became my dream. And because of my strength of purpose, it never seemed impossible. No, actually it seemed very possible. Though it was invisible, I could see it in my mind and feel it in my heart. When I told people about it, they thought: *That's just another kid talking.* It is hard for some people to believe in something they can't see. I was the only one who could see it, until it became a reality.

I learned to play lead guitar, and I got a job at the Illuminating Company, where I worked for twenty-three years. Father's Dream Appliances began while I was still working there, with two old stoves I found on the street. I picked them up, bought a DIY repair manual for $7.95 and fixed them up, making them look new.

Soon I had enough appliances to open a small store. The day I opened, I saw a man walking down the street and politely asked him if he'd like to see something. "Sure," he said. I brought him in and proudly showed him all my appliances. "You brought me in here to show me *appliances?*" he said. "Nobody cares about that." That almost made me believe I was on the wrong track. But shortly after that, a man came in and bought a stove for two hundred dollars. This turned me around. I saw that dreams really *do* come true.

I attended the West Side Institute of Technology while working at the Illuminating Company and starting the appliance business. In my heating and air conditioning class one day, my teacher had said, "Keep coming. Keep coming. Soon, there will come a moment when you understand everything." But one afternoon, I was so tired I just walked out. I got home, got comfortable, and a voice told me to go back. With eight kids and two jobs, my father had never had a chance to go. What would he think of me if I quit? I went back, and sure enough, that was the night that I understood everything the teacher was saying. In that moment, I was so close to quitting—and so close to accomplishing my goal. Somehow the path became clear: Keep my father, the dream and the promise in mind.

The Almighty called my father home just when I had really become my father's best friend and was able to start giving back to him—just before he would have had the chance to see Father's Dream Appliances occupy a nine-thousand-square-foot store fronting on East 93rd Street. Nor was he able to see the second,

> *In that moment, I was so close to quitting—and so close to accomplishing my goal. Somehow the path became clear: Keep my father, the dream and the promise in mind.*

twenty-thousand-square-foot store I opened on Woodland Avenue. My mom got to see one of them, though. I advertised on the sides of shopping carts in ten major grocery stores in Cleveland, Ohio, and before my mom passed, she loved to go into the stores just to push the carts around and say, "That's my son!"

Every step of the way, my father celebrated my accomplishments and set me new tasks on the road to fulfilling what had become our dream. People asked me why I worked so hard, getting up at four a.m. every day. I told them about my strength of purpose, and how all my actions are dedicated to my father. How it meant knowing I was not just on the right track but the right train. I had wondered at times if there would ever be time for my own dreams. But living my father's dreams for him showed me I could live mine. That was his ultimate gift: serendipity. Serendipity is discovering something good from doing something good.

All this is why I am here today with a new dream: to go all over the world, sharing my story and letting people know that dreams really do come true. You may not be able to see or understand ninety-five percent of your journey, but if you work hard every

> *Sometimes you will get tired. But you'll draw strength from your purpose, and it will give you energy to start all over again. And your dream will become a train you just can't stop.*

day toward your dream, and keep your strength of purpose clearly in front of you, as I did with my father's voice and image, the Almighty will make every provision to help you reach your goals. Trust yourself. Earl Nightingale said, "Everyone living is meant to live. The universe is no accident, we are no accident. We all have a purpose."

We may not know why we're born, what we should do, or why we have the goals we do—but we need to know that our goals are sentimental. They should be emotional. I've learned that hard work is not the key to success, it's the reason why we're doing it. Success is a matter of finding yourself and building upon what you find. So, see your dream in your mind, and feel it in your heart. Learn to trust in yourself and your higher power as I learned to trust my father when he had me touch those two wires.

Sometimes you will get tired. But you'll draw strength from your purpose, and it will give you energy to start all over again. And your dream will become a train you just can't stop. It will keep looking at you and refuse to look away. So never give up. When you get so close, often you don't realize how close you are. Sometimes it takes just one more step, and you're there. Your stamina always relates to your strength of purpose. One day, you'll wonder where it all came from. After learning to be a go-getter, you will become a go-giver.

My father always seems to visit me, in everything I do. He is my ancestor, my touchstone, my teacher. And when I look in the mirror, I see him. He is always a part of me. No matter what I do, I always ask myself, "Would my father be proud of this? What would he think?" That's the strength of the purpose.

Over thirty-nine years ago, Reginald Alfonzo Sizemore began his quest to accomplish his father's, John Perry Sizemore's, dreams. Having accomplished all four, he is now an experienced entrepreneur, guitarist, graduate of West Side Institute of Technology and an appliance technician and grade one electrician who worked at the Illuminating Company for twenty-three years. Reginald has assisted more than twenty-thousand customers. They purchase appliances and stay to talk about their dreams and goals. They want the details on how, thanks to his promise to his father, Reginald created Father's Dream Appliances in Cleveland, Ohio, and succeeded, against the odds, in building a small African-American-owned business into a success. Reginald was exposed to motivational products at the age of fifteen and began his lifelong quest to follow his own dream and become a professional public speaker to help, encourage and share his message with others to follow their dreams— because dreams really do come true. Connect with Reginald at www.ReginaldASizemore.com.

Debi Donner

THE OLYMPICS OF THE HEART AND SOUL

I magine you and your partner living in total harmony. All your wants and needs are satisfied, and every morning when you wake up, you look over at your partner's face and feel a deep connection and genuine love.

If this sounds like a pipe dream to you right now, don't despair. The happy relationship I'm describing is absolutely possible. You simply have to commit to training for it by building a core foundation of great communication skills that will help you get through the hard times, even those moments that feel like real breaking points, times when it seems you and your partner will *never* understand each other. "Communication" is a broad word, especially these days. Many of us spend all day communicating via email, instant messaging, text messaging, voicemail, Skype, Twitter and FaceBook, but we are in the dark when it comes to more intimate communication and the interpersonal challenges it creates. But it doesn't have to be that way.

First of all, being a less-than-perfect communicator is nothing to be ashamed of. Successful, empathic interpersonal communication, especially between men and women, is not something most of us are taught. What we need to bring to the table is not denial, refusal or some unattainable ideal of perfection; what we need most to really succeed is a *desire* to communicate, a willingness to try, a willingness to learn. If we're lucky enough to be raised in a setting where conscious communication takes place between our parents, *some* of that can rub off on us as kids. But regardless of our circumstances, communication skills need to—and can—be developed and strengthened throughout our lives, just like muscles in the body.

As a life coach working primarily with healing the long lineage of misunderstandings, limiting beliefs, miscommunication and wounding between women and men in relationships, I've seen that, almost without exception, if each half of a duo is willing to work on building his or her communication muscles, real breakthroughs can be achieved.

> *But regardless of our circumstances, communication skills need to—and can—be developed and strengthened throughout our lives, just like muscles in the body.*

As with any exercise, you work to build muscle and with any relationship you work to build great communication skills. It's like training for the Olympics of the heart and soul. It may be tough at first, but nothing could be more rewarding. And the more you train, the stronger you get. That way when a crisis hits, you already have the skills to handle it, rather than having the rug pulled out from under you. This determination to build strength has paid off for me a hundred times over in relationships. It has also worked for me literally: before I found my path as a life coach and speaker, I was totally dedicated to my life as an athlete, bodybuilder and fitness competitor.

I was stocky and a bit chunky growing up. As a cheerleader, I was always used as the base for other girls to climb up on. My mom's terms of endearment were not always so polite; she constantly pointed out my chubby imperfections, while my grandma always graciously tried to protect me and my feelings by saying, "Oh that's nothing, that's just baby fat, you'll grow out of it."

As an adult, I was determined to not only lose that weight, but to get into the best shape I possibly could. I became an aerobics instructor and then a fitness competitor, training my heart out and winning first place titles from the Midwest to the West Coast. I was featured in magazines and commercials as an athlete and a fitness model. After competing in the Fitness America Pageant and placing sixth out of one hundred and fifty-seven women, I was thrilled and awestruck. To celebrate, I went on a cruise with my friends. After the cruise, I decided to take one last photo as we waited for our charter bus.

I crossed the street and stood behind a van with an attached trailer. I was lining up and focusing on my picture when the van started and took off. The trailer knocked me to the ground and somehow I was dragged along with it. If I hadn't been dragged, I would have been run over. I heard my friends screaming. They ran after the van, banging on the vehicle to get the driver to stop.

I was a disaster: torn rotator cuff, dislocated hip, soft tissue damage, cuts, abrasions, stitches and bandages everywhere. The paramedics told me that if I hadn't been in such good shape, I never would have walked away from the accident. A short while later, after my first physical therapy session, I was rear-ended by a drunk driver and injured further. Recovery was a struggle, and I became depressed from chronic pain and being unable to use my body as I had. Though I will not compete again, I do have my body back. But I may never have recovered from that severe setback if I hadn't already committed to building my own strength.

Communication between couples works the same way. If your communication skills are well developed, your relationship will be strong enough to get through—even grow through—traumatic life events, like disagreements that constantly hit a brick wall, ultimatums, arguments over finances, infidelity, a serious illness or the death of a parent.

Where serious communication issues are present, these events often lead to a break or divorce, because someone changed, because the partners don't know how to reach an agreeable solution or because they don't have the skills to empathize with or talk to each other. When this is the case, problems that had been skated past may seem extremely overwhelming during really tough life transitions.

Most men are more verbally direct: they say what they mean, and mean what they say. Women, on the other hand, tend not to voice our needs and wants; we're always trying to be accommodating and supportive. We won't speak directly, but we have great expectations of our men, wanting them to be mind-readers when

> *We all speak different love languages, but we can also learn to embrace and understand our differences. This can open us up to enormous potential growth.*

they tend instead to work at the task at hand, trying to complete the job. When a woman speaks, she wants to be heard. When a man listens, he wants to fix the problem. But she's not looking for the solution to the problem, she's looking for comfort. The comfort is in the listening, not in the solution.

One client of mine feels bombarded by his wife every time he walks in the door after work and she tells him about what happened that day, how the kids got into trouble and what problem is occurring with the house. He's just worked his butt off all day, and needs to be affirmed in order to believe his efforts are worthwhile. She's been attending, meanwhile, to all the other realms of life, and needs him to hear her, needs his participation in the family. He shuts down and retreats to his cave, while she—again—gets very upset that he isn't paying attention to her. Both partners feel neglected by the other.

We all speak different love languages, but we can also learn to embrace and understand our differences. This can open us up to enormous potential growth. With awareness of each other's love languages, these two are able to finally communicate. She has learned to affirm the value of his work when he comes home: "I am so grateful for and appreciative of what you do for me and our family—you are the greatest." In response, she gets the warmth, emotional support and quality time she wants from and with him.

In addition to becoming familiar with your own love language, and your partner's, one of the greatest things you can do to strengthen your communication muscle is to *not interrupt*. Let your loved one finish his thoughts and get his feelings out, or they'll stay locked inside. Resentment and eruptions occur when what

> *A relationship is strong if you feel good in it.*

needs to be said doesn't come out. You'll be amazed at what gold you can discover when you and your partner both feel listened to and cared for. "People will forget what you said, people will forget what you did," writes Maya Angelou, "but people will never forget how you made them feel."

A relationship is strong if you feel good in it. When your partner speaks, listen. Don't interrupt. Then, repeat what you just heard him say. At first, shockingly, you will discover that most of the time what you heard and what he said are two different things. But when a real effort is being made between you to actually hear and understand each other, it will get easier with practice. Your emotional responsiveness will strengthen your emotional bond and help heal what is wounded in your relationship.

Most people in a relationship want to know: Are you there for me? Do I matter to you? Will you come when I need you? Do you love me for who I am? Great communication answers "yes" to all these questions in the most fundamental, enduring way. A kind of relationship training, communication takes work and dedication every day, but the strength it brings to your core being and your relationship is more than worth the sweat.

As a life coach, Debi Donner is passionate about helping you realize your potential and supporting you to take action in manifesting your goals, dreams and desires. She is an inspirational and motivational speaker, personal and professional life coach and an Executive Coach for Impact Consulting & Development (founded by Dr. Todd Thomas, world-renowned speaker, author, trainer and coach). Debi is a Coach Consultant for NLPCA out of San Francisco, California, and is a member of the Les Brown Platinum Speakers Network. She holds a BS in business management and has an extensive background in psychology. Additional training includes an intensive self-development course with the Hoffman Institute and the PAX Programs Inc.'s Mastery and Leadership Program, focused on learning, understanding and celebrating the differences between men and women. Debi focuses on helping others create and maintain strong relationships as a key to success and happiness. Visit Transformations By Debi at www.DebiDonner.com.

Robert Vitelli

THERE IS NO FAILURE, ONLY FEEDBACK

I was at my dad's house in Jersey one weekend night watching TV when the phone rang. I jumped up to answer it—it was my mom. Her voice sounded very strange. "You're going to be staying with your dad, honey," she said. "Mommy's going to heaven tonight. I just wanted to say goodbye." Though I was only eight, I knew instantly what that meant. Mom had been severely depressed for a long time; she was a stressed-out single mom, running herself ragged working seventy-five hours a week and in a pretty unhealthy relationship to boot.

"Dad," I shouted, panicked. "I think Mom's trying to kill herself." He rushed to the phone. "Are you okay? What's going on?" he asked. I heard her crying on the other line. "Stay where you are. You're going to be all right." He hung up with my mom and immediately called 911. An ambulance rushed to our apartment in New York just in time; she had downed several bottles of prescription medication. They pumped her stomach and just barely saved her life. I spent the next ten years trying to save my mom from hurting. In our codependent relationship, I was the enabler— her support system, her cuddle-machine, the one to bring her up whenever she felt down.

Instead of being driven to self-destruct as a teenager, I became deeply motivated to work on myself. I started reading motivational literature, and at the age of twenty, I attended my first personal growth seminar with Brian Tracy. I saw my dad occasionally, but I didn't have a role model, or a mentor. So I was always seeking to fill that void within me, always looking for someone to show me the road to success.

Fast-forward to my mid-twenties, when I was experiencing an incredible level of financial success. Traveling the country, tossing money to the wind, I was living in an atmosphere of fame and glamour. But I was also completely miserable. I was working seventy hours per week and my health was deteriorating

> *I saw my dad occasionally, but I didn't have a role model, or a mentor. So I was always seeking to fill that void within me, always looking for someone to show me the road to success.*

rapidly. One night, while I was driving cross-country through Nebraska with my girlfriend, the car in front of us lost control and started flipping end over end. We pulled over and ran to the car; its two passengers had been killed instantly. Their ruined bodies hung from the doors. We called 911, and waited for the ambulance.

In shock, we drove a little further to a motel, and stopped for the night to decompress. We turned on the TV and *Frankie and Johnny* was on. Halfway through the movie, I broke down and started bawling my eyes out. It freaked out my girlfriend—it kind of flipped me out, too. But this was the first time I'd ever seen people die, and it made me re-evaluate, instantly, what was important to me. "What's wrong?" she asked. "I'm miserable," I answered.

I'd bought into the myth of money and fame, and what had it brought me? This gig was a sure two to three million a year, and I'd be looking at double that the next year. But I wasn't enjoying my life. I was exhausted, I had no friends, and I felt no joy. My greed-based mentality had led me to a desolate place. And I realized: *I'm doing just what Mom did.* Unconsciously, I was sabotaging myself by duplicating her patterns.

In the days that followed, I quit my job. My lifestyle had come with massive overhead expenses, and I was forced to claim bankruptcy. I gave my BMW back to the bank and bought a Ford Fiesta for a couple hundred bucks. Living at the financial bottom of the barrel, I felt an enormous new sense of freedom and possibility. And that's when I decided, with a ferocious resolve, to study every personal growth technique and modality I could get my hands on to see what really worked.

For years, I studied with the biggest motivational speakers and transformational-thought leaders from around the world. I also worked for Jim Rohn, Zig Ziglar and Brian Tracy, teaching and promoting their seminars. Piecing together what worked one hundred percent of the time from all these different sources;

> *One of the major lessons I learned in my journey is that there is no failure—only results and feedback.*

throwing away the fluff; combining hypnosis, psychology, neurolinquistics, somatic psychology and body work, I developed a transformational system of my own. My income went from ten to fifteen thousand to over a hundred thousand a month! But this time, things were completely different. This time, I was living a happy, balanced life, free from the inherited reaction patterns that had caused my previous misery. One of the major lessons I learned in my journey is that there is no failure—only results and feedback.

But in the beginning, even working with affirmations and positive thinking, I used to beat myself up. I was still having an internal, subconscious reaction: "Oh, man, I suck!" That judgment of failure was only a habitual point of view, an inherited critical reaction pattern that I took on from the major role model in my life—my mother. But I didn't know that at the time. In the deepest part of myself, I took it as truth.

We all take on such patterns in order to survive. And occasionally, they help us succeed *beyond* the realm of childhood survival. But unfortunately, most people don't realize their dreams because of these unconscious reaction patterns. The results caused by unconscious reaction patterns are usually of the unwanted variety. And ninety-nine percent of us don't even know we have these unconscious patterns and blocks to joy, freedom, wealth and success.

It's important to prioritize working on yourself, but the trouble is, you can't consciously work on something you are unconscious of. It's impossible! You may know your relationship is a mess, your bank account is in the red and your job is from hell, but by definition, unconscious blocks are those you cannot uncover on

> *Positive thinking is wonderful, but using affirmations to work with subconscious blocks is like giving a random medication to someone with a serious illness and hoping it works to cure them.*

your own. Ask someone what her subconscious blocks are, and she simply will not be able to tell you. Positive thinking is wonderful, but using affirmations to work with subconscious blocks is like giving a random medication to someone with a serious illness and hoping it works to cure them.

So you may rally. But your unaddressed reaction patterns will sabotage you every time. Success cannot last if the pattern has not been removed. These patterns also show up in our physical body structure, our posture and the way we move. Some of these behaviors are obvious to an onlooker, but many of them are very subtle micro-behaviors. These minute micro-behaviors, combined with the larger, more obvious ones, usually create the opposite result than what we are consciously going after in the various areas of life!

For example: The most powerful people I've met are also the most perceptive. When you walk into a room, they read you like a book: they pick up on the micro-behaviors, opinions, thoughts and beliefs that come through in your voice, your physical habits and the way you walk, reflecting your unconscious patterns. Your neurology is ALWAYS reflected in your physiology. And when you identify and eliminate these unconscious reaction patterns, your feelings, emotions AND physiology change accordingly. The messages you project begin to lead you toward the results you actually want.

If you're ready to get off your unconscious rollercoaster, the first thing you have to do is become aware of these inherited reaction patterns and STOP THEM in their tracks! Introspection alone isn't going to do it; you need to find a mentor or a teacher whom you can trust and respect enough to show you your unconscious patterns and support you in eliminating them fast.

These days, I'm experiencing a tremendous level of joy, balance and wholeness. I enjoy great health, friendships and prosperity— not working myself to death in an unconscious duplication of my mother's self-destructive behavior, but making a difference in the world and adding value to millions of people's lives through doing what I have an absolute passion for.

How great it feels to trust completely, now that I have cleared these patterns from my own life, that I'll never sabotage myself again! And the elegant flip side to my *codependent* pattern is, I'm great at empowering and supporting others. That invaluable information has made dreams come true for me and countless others.

For the past twenty-four years, Robert Vitelli has been a pioneer in the field of human potential. He is the author and creator of the groundbreaking new book and personal growth technology, Being The Powerful You!™ *and recently co-authored* Pushing To The Front *with personal growth legend Brian Tracy.*

As well as being a leading authority on personal mastery, Robert is also a world-class speaker who delivers inspirational presentations around the world and intimately understands the dynamics and desired outcomes of live events. His dramatic and entertaining storytelling combined with his unique ability to connect with an audience and intuitively speak to its subconscious needs is beyond extraordinary. Robert is regularly sought out by industry experts, organizations and companies to share and speak about his breakthrough techniques and strategies, and he has appeared in national papers as well as on network television. Connect with Robert at www.RobertVitelli.com.

Vanessa McLean

THE DOORWAY OF DESIRE

Coming to the United Kingdom from Jamaica in 1952 as a young couple, my parents faced incredible racism, discrimination and abuse in the pursuit of their dream: a better life for their family. I was blessed to have such wise, dedicated, generous and loving parents, who taught me the importance of holding onto my dream in every action they took and in every word they spoke.

Growing up in Jamaica, my father lost both his parents by the time he was eleven and had to leave school at twelve to provide and care for his little brothers and sisters. Thanks to his strong will and character, he managed to do this *and* own a farm and a store by the time he was a young man. After he met my mother, they decided to emigrate to the United Kingdom and work there for five years. They hoped this would be enough time to raise money for their future children's education and to help support their families back home.

My father arrived in London with hopes for a rosy future, but was met with a series of slammed doors. People regarded him as no better than an animal. In a city where most lodging-houses had signs out front that read, "No coloreds, no Irish, no dogs," my parents went from street to street, door to door, searching for a place to live. It was hard, but they kept knocking on doors.

Their desire and their determination not to give up finally paid off. Sharing rooms with other families, working hard, my parents bought their first home six years later, a six-bedroom house. They helped other relatives to come to the United Kingdom as well.

My father intended to go back home within five years. It was not until twenty-five years later that he returned to his beloved Jamaica—for a visit, not to live. London had become his home. The greater dream of creating opportunities for his children had been realized, and he showed us that although his dream of return had not been achieved, he had not given up on it. An upright, robust and hardworking man, he taught us honor, respect and integrity. "It doesn't matter where you are," he'd say. "Work with what you've got." Perhaps most importantly, he inspired us to believe that we could achieve anything.

My mother was—and still is—my greatest inspiration. Due to medical negligence, she was left unable to walk for many years. And though she never got better, she never got bitter. I never heard her indulge in self-pity. She had such strength, such humility. Full of compassion, love for God, life and people, she welcomed everyone into her home and embraced them as her own children and family.

My mother always had the right words to share with people, encouraging, uplifting and empowering them. Her words of love and warmth helped give them—and me—direction and purpose. After she became disabled, her bed became her platform, and her bedside telephone became her microphone.

She gave so much of herself. Someone visiting our home would ask her how she was, and she'd say, "Oh, thank God for glory, I could be worse!"

This amazing woman was unable to walk, and took pain-relieving medication twenty-four hours a day—and yet she was thanking God for her life and the love in it at every possible moment. It was always a pure, uplifting joy to be in her presence. The core essence of life is love, and that is one of the other great gifts I got from my parents—especially my mother.

Everyone who met her would say they wished they had a mother or an auntie like her. And I knew then: *I want to be like that when I get older.* I wanted to have an impact on people the way my mother did. That was the first piece of my purpose—my "why"—to fall into place.

I had never thought of myself as a speaker; in fact, I was always considered shy and reserved outside of one-to-one conversations. As the youngest of four children, I'd suffered from low self-esteem and always deferred to my eloquent older sister. I stepped back, wallflower-like, and let her do all the speaking, but deep inside, I

> *I didn't realize that, years later, the blessing would come in discovering the gift of my voice and carrying on my mother's legacy. It felt so good to give back to my parents, and all of the difficulties I faced at that time showed me what I was made of. I finally came into my own.*

dreamed of a great future. I had a burning desire to live abroad and become an extremely successful entrepreneur. I just didn't have the confidence to express it yet.

When I was in my late twenties, my parents became ill, and I spent a lot of time caring for them. Two days before my father's death, he called me into his room and said, "Vanessa, you are the last of my four children—you have had it really hard. You could have led your own life; you could have married. You have done so much for us. But don't worry, God is going to bless you." I left the room with copious tears streaming down my cheeks. When my mother passed away six months later, I was devastated. I didn't realize that, years later, the blessing would come in discovering the gift of my voice and carrying on my mother's legacy. It felt so good to give back to my parents, and all of the difficulties I faced at that time showed me what I was made of. I finally came into my own.

In 2002, I went to Ghana and met the children there who had so little, but were so grateful for what they had. Their openness and generosity to me moved me deeply. Back in England, it was a completely different way of life. I knew I had to give back, to do something for these children.

That was and is another huge piece of my "why." Every day I wake up thinking about it, and every day I'm getting closer. I didn't know how I was going to swing it financially back then, but now, because I have stayed committed to my dream, the universe is putting people and opportunities in my path to help me realize my dream in Africa.

> *If you're going to give someone else so much of your time—commit to them, work for them—why not make that commitment to yourself? What about your dream?*

And then, about four years ago, I began giving presentations and was bitten by the speaking bug. It was a delightful surprise. All the years of feeling shy vanished. When I saw the effect I was having on people, I knew I'd hit upon my real life's purpose, and my truest dream. The burning desire to help others transform their lives through words of love and encouragement, as my mother did, gave me the confidence to recognize that I've got a voice, and my voice needs to be heard.

Speaking has led me to face and unleash my fear; it certainly took me out of my comfort zone. But when I touch someone's heart, when I see tears of hope rolling down peoples' faces because my story has moved them, any fear left over is illuminated for what it is: simply fear. Once a woman who had listened to me speak about finding my own voice approached me to explain how deeply my message had resonated with her. "You don't realize," she said, "you've given me life." I thought: *There's no better feeling in the world for me, no better measure of success.*

You too have a big dream simmering inside you. You possess incredible gifts, a wellspring of talent to share with the world. And of course you don't want your dream to exist simply as a wish. So how do you make your dream come true?

To make your dream a reality, you need to fuel it with pure passion, a burning desire that carries you, with gathering momentum, toward what you love. You need to have a WHY. Your "why" is your purpose, the reason you get out of bed every morning and make another step toward your dream. It infuses you with the strength you need to keep knocking on doors until the right one opens.

So many people have so much to share—but sadly, they may not even be conscious that they have given up on their dream. Maybe they're living someone else's dream, and have become unhappy and unfulfilled in the process. Maybe their "whys" come from somewhere outside. So many people destroy their

> *Never give up. Keep your commitment to your commitment, and keep knocking on those doors. Your dream is real, and precious, and deserves all your passion.*

souls by forfeiting their dreams every day when they go to work. A paycheck is only enough for us to keep coming back the next day, the next month. Our "why" has to keep us coming back our whole life long. If you're going to give someone else so much of your time—commit to them, work for them—why not make that commitment to yourself? What about *your* dream?

My mother always said to me, "You've got to place a value on your life." And she'd often remind me, "You are a precious diamond." I place a huge value on my life. Far too often we don't see ourselves for what we're worth. We lose in life because we're prepared to eat crumbs rather than feast at the banquet—but we *are* enough. We are more than enough, and we can achieve anything. It's about desire. How much do I desire the change? How much passion have I got to go after my dream? Is it worth it?

There's more to life than getting by. Your "why" has to be as big as you are, and guide you through the tough times, as my parents' dream of a new life for their children kept them intact and happy while doors were being slammed all around them. They were rewarded for never giving up—and so are we all. Find your "why," and give it all you have. Your unflagging desire will not fail to create doorways to your dream. And the positive feedback you receive, once you commit to your dream, is extraordinary. Never give up. Keep your commitment to your commitment, and keep knocking on those doors. Your dream is real, and precious, and deserves all your passion.

Before I go onstage, I always pray, and give thanks that I had two great parents who left a wonderful legacy in me of perseverance and love. I'll share their love. I share that wherever I go. There are no guarantees in life but my own commitment to that goal—and that's exactly right.

Vanessa McLean is the co-founder of the Voice Alignment Network (www.VoiceAlignmentNetwork.com), an organization that helps people discover their authentic voice. Trained by motivational speaker Les Brown, she is an inspirational speaker whose audiences are always captivated, moved and challenged to fulfill their full potential. Coming to and from the heart in her soft, melodious voice, Vanessa's eloquent and compassionate delivery accentuates her messages to the world about having a big dream, overcoming fear and embracing possibility. Learn more about Vanessa's work at www.VanessaMcLean.com and www.UnleashTheFear.com.

Ela Corcoran

THE DREAM THAT HEALS ALL OTHERS

The moment I stepped off the plane in Hawaii, I knew I had made the right decision. The air was soft, pure and sweet, and everywhere I looked I found a different, beautiful shade of green. This was a healing place. I had left everything behind, all the pressures of family and career, to get well. I took a deep, cleansing breath. And with it, I finally allowed my healing process to begin.

Doctors had informed me some time before that I had a very rare type of breast cancer known as Paget's Disease. I wasn't surprised. Ever since I had graduated from homeopathy school, I'd had a feeling something wasn't right—I just didn't know what it was. I'd changed my diet and treated myself homeopathically since long before the diagnosis, but something more needed to be done. I knew my life was out of balance.

Even after the diagnosis, though, I did not take bolder steps with my health. I was radically stressed. My dad was ill and dying in Poland, and I visited frequently to care for him. I was working non-stop in my homeopathic career, and was in the middle of moving from England back to the States. When my dad finally passed away on 9-11, his funeral was postponed for a week because my brother and I were in the States, and all flights out had been cancelled. My grief was intense—both personal and national.

My decision not to tell my family and friends about my illness was deliberate. I knew my family would not have been able to provide emotional support and that their negativity would be a burden. My mom's expression of love is to worry, and I did not need the added stress. I had left Poland because of that dark outlook. To me, it seemed embedded in the culture after so many years of suffering and war. But the real reason I didn't speak out was that I felt I had failed. I had helped so many people, I'd been there for them as a doctor, a daughter, a friend—but I had not been there for myself.

After years as a holistic practitioner and student of personal development, here I was, ill and non-functional at some level. I was very disappointed with myself.

My diagnosis was less frightening to me, though, than what the doctors suggested for treatment. It was the typical, invasive Western approach to cancer—surgery, radiation. Nobody told me to change my diet. They never even asked me what I was eating.

> But the real reason I didn't speak out was that I felt I had failed. I had helped so many people, I'd been there for them as a doctor, a daughter, a friend—but I had not been there for myself.

Nobody asked me what had been going on in my life. "We will have to investigate," they told me. I didn't want to be probed or cut open. "You are not touching it," I told them. I would do it my own way.

I had already changed my diet and implemented a routine of homeopathic remedies, but I really needed to get away from my stressful life. I was still working and traveling too much. After my father died, my mother had come from Poland to live with me. My stress level increased even more. It wasn't until after further tests that I made my big move. I saw the fright on my doctors' faces when they looked at my results. "This is it," they said. "Do something now, or you won't make it." Overnight, all my other dreams and commitments—career, family, travel—became secondary to my dream of rebuilding my health and staying alive. I needed to escape.

I needed to be in someplace beautiful, green and tranquil in a natural, healing environment far from all my stress. Hawaii, a dream place, came to mind. I formed a clear picture of an ideal location just waiting for me there. One morning, I awoke knowing I needed to make a contact in Hawaii right away. I remembered a friend I'd met a year earlier, who lived on the Big Island, and emailed her. Although she rarely checked her emails, she did that day. She responded, "How perfect that you contacted me today! I just heard about a small house on an eighty-acre farm that might be available."

I rented out my condo, sent my mother to stay with my brother, closed my homeopathic practice, packed my bags and flew to Hawaii. Everyone thought I was going on a long vacation. On the plane, I instantly felt my burdens leaving me. No work, no patients, no family—this was the time for me to heal myself. This was a purposeful trip. There was no question: I would get well.

I stayed on the Big Island, on a vast, remote lychee farm filled with trees and singing birds. Every day I breathed that wonderful, healing air as I did my energizing exercises, meditation and yoga. I ate beautiful food. Twice a week, the farmer drove me to the town market, where I bought fresh fruits and vegetables. Focusing on my gratitude for life, I made everything a ritual and a celebration. And that left no room for negative thoughts about my illness or for negative people. Solitude was cleansing. The farmer's dog, a Rottweiler named Yogi, often joined me on my walks and swims in the waterfalls.

It was a beautiful time for me. Eventually, life called me back to the mainland. After six months of a stress-free life and nurturing self-care, I had regained my health. A blood test showed that the cancer markers— and the lesions on my body that had been a sign of my cancer—were all gone. Thermography, a less invasive alternative to a mammogram, also showed that the cancer was gone. Most importantly, I knew I was well. I don't believe that I actually *did* anything when it came to my healing. I only facilitated it. I allowed myself to receive the healing.

Sometimes we want to be healed but don't allow healing to occur. We're probably not even aware of when we make that decision. It's not always happening on a conscious level. Sometimes it seems as

> *If people give your dream a dire prognosis, don't let it lead you into doubt. Never give up, no matter what.*

if regaining our health is out of our hands, that it's a pipe dream. But illness is a transgression against health laws. We create our illness, but we can make ourselves well by returning to a life lived according to those laws.

A new dream grows from each dream realized, but I'd forgotten that all of my dreams were contingent upon following my dream of regaining vibrant health. My prayers and persistence had guided me back to a place where I could materialize it—and the truth is, you have the power to bring any dream into reality. Everything begins with a vision, a picture in your mind, like my picture of the healing dream-place. You have to visit often to make it real. No dream will come to us if it is not possible to achieve.

If people give your dream a dire prognosis, don't let it lead you into doubt. Never give up, no matter what. When we doubt, that internal voice we listen to is often not really our intuition; it is merely the accumulated voices of our past, our parents, our teachers. If you want something and it doesn't work out, it doesn't mean that it isn't possible, only that it might not be possible *at this moment*. And if your beliefs tell you something is impossible, it's impossible.

We all have blockages, feelings that hold us back. We cannot measure the energy that blocks us, so we name it, calling it anger, sadness or frustration. But feelings are merely vibrations, and if we change those feelings, we can change the energy, and the blockages will disappear. It's not we who really heal, it's that power that we allow ourselves to access that heals. Medical treatment is a gift God has provided us, and whatever method we believe in will serve us and help us. But nothing is as perfect as approaching that power and asking for help. You will always find the right answer there.

> *In the end, what you strive for is not as important as who you become during the process.*

That kind of clarity, the same kind I accessed in Hawaii, leads to feelings of true happiness and true dream fulfillment. That is why it is so important to search for and discover what your purpose in life truly is. It is the starting point for all our successes. You are never the same person as you were before you step into power and onto the path that leads to your dreams. In the end, what you strive for is not as important as who you become during the process.

My healing experience brought me more confidence when helping others to get well. I know from experience, now, that they can do it, too. It made me more compassionate, more understanding and a better person. I love myself more. And I'm so grateful to finally have the opportunity to share the story of my fight and victory with you, and with my family.

Whether you receive this story as an empowering tool or the sound of a voice in the wilderness, I am happy to share it with you. And I want to hear your story, too. The greater the number of us holding our images and sharing our stories, the greater the chance for our dreams to take wing and fly!

Born in Poland, Ela Corcoran is a holistic health practitioner, coach and enterpreneur. She has been practicing homeopathic medicine for over fifteen years. After graduating from the College of Homeopathy in London and completing post-graduate advanced study as a homeopathic physician at Bengal Allen Medical Institute in India, she studied and practiced extensively with some of the world's leading homeopaths in the United States, England, India, Greece, Germany, Belgium and France. She holds two master's degrees and numerous certifications in various other healing methods including energy psychology, Emotional Freedom Technique (EFT), nutrition, different paths of yoga, meditation and various technologies on the vibrational medicine frontier. She specializes in anti-aging.

Ela has been trained by one of the top success coaches in the industry, Bob Proctor. Becoming a certified LifeSuccess Consultant has now put her in a position to fulfill her lifelong dream of helping others through coaching. As a coach and holistic health practitioner, Ela aims to help her clients achieve freedom from limitations in their lives and ultimately maintain their own health to prevent all illness. If you are facing a health challenge or want to be proactive in achieving and maintaining true youthfulness, connect with Ela at www.ElaCorcoran.com

Remi Duyile

DREAMING
STRATEGICALLY

Everyone has a dream. And when we're young, though we might not know ourselves very well yet, we still unconsciously pursue our dreams by gravitating toward the things that give us the most joy. Later, as adults, our dreams require conscious pursuit, a solid strategy to move us from point A to point B that is centered in real self-knowledge, self-acceptance, nurturance and connection with the wider world around us.

As a young girl coming of age in Nigeria, I was very impressed with the way professional women in my community—particularly the bankers—carried themselves. They were elegant, well dressed and walked with an air of confidence and credibility I admired. My older sister, a principal health educator for the government and an educationist, was one of many strong female role models in my life. I witnessed the process of her emergence as a leader in her male-dominated profession—which she did with deliberation, style, grace and balance—and realized that I too could be whatever I wanted to be.

I wanted to be a banker. At first it was mostly because of those women I'd seen, their elegant dress and self-assuredness. Later, in my teens, as I learned more about the world, I realized that banking was pivotal in society, and how essential financial matters are to everyone's life. I enjoyed working with numbers, and I loved working with people.

So, at seventeen, I immigrated to the United States to study business, staying with my brother and his family, who gave me invaluable support as I worked hard in school and to acclimate to a whole new way of life. Within five years, I earned an MBA. Right out of school, I got a job as a bank teller. Pursuing a very specific strategy, I fought for and eventually reached my goal of becoming a Vice President with Bank of America. This process took about ten years, and it wasn't always easy. At times it didn't even seem possible. But I never thought, not even for one day, of giving it up. All along, I was on a mission.

There's an essential process we all have to go through in order to realize our dream, a core of empowerment to build. There's really nothing mysterious about it, or out of reach, as long as you use a simple strategy that begins with knowing who you are, going to the innermost depths and identifying your uniqueness. Who you are is essential to the world, but you're not going to be able to offer it up if you don't know yourself.

A very significant piece of knowing yourself involves finding your passion. What *is* your dream? To find the passion that will drive and sustain you, keep aligning yourself with the things you like to do by investigating ways in which you can be of service. I call this "strategic volunteerism"—it not only furthers your development and shows you your own strength, it contributes to the community. A true understanding of who you are, and what your passion and purpose are, are not enough to realize your dream. The next strategic step is to really embrace your uniqueness, no matter who else sees and values it.

It may come as a surprise to many that I wanted to work as a bank teller when I had an MBA. But I was there on a specific mission. I wanted to learn the basics, and start networking from the bottom up. I was also aware that there were certain "strikes" against me that I would have to *disprove* as strikes by developing a long track record of superior results, so starting out as a teller was a simple strategy for entering the company. When I moved to America from Africa, everything changed. Being black, African and female, with a foreign accent on top of it, I simultaneously stuck out and was tuned out altogether by most people.

But those "strikes" were things I was proud of. And they were things I could not change. So I had to immediately accept and embrace them, or I would never have been able to survive. I had to learn to move beyond my upset when people didn't see or accept

> *A true understanding of who you are, and what your passion and purpose are, are not enough to realize your dream. The next strategic step is to really embrace your uniqueness, no matter who else sees and values it.*

me, when they behaved with malice or insensitivity; I even learned to joke to myself about the security cameras that were constantly trained on me (being African, foreign, I was watched perpetually), and to speak slowly so people could understand my accent.

I was even told, when I was hired, that I was "too dressed for the building." "Who do you think you are?" was the subtext. But I still held that vision of my sister and all the other elegant businesswomen I had admired growing up. They always looked professional, no matter what their job was. I took my five-hundred-dollar credit card and bought suits. What my bosses and colleagues didn't know—and I did—was that I was dressing for my future; I was on my mission, and just passing through. And I kept focused on being the best, knowing that as I continued to deliver results, the results could not be argued with. My value couldn't be ignored, even if they wanted to.

We all encounter what I call "vision-killers" on the path to our dream: those people who will find a way to discourage you, especially if you have a positive attitude, or who offer five hundred reasons why your dream will never happen—because it never happened for them. They'll spread gossip: "Did you hear what the boss said about you yesterday during lunch?" They want you to have a negative attitude around people who are going to be responsible for your future. They'll rub in your strikes: "Don't be too quick to forget where you come from," they'll say, in a friendly way, but when you leave them you find your head hanging down.

This is simply a sign that you're talking to the wrong people. If you're coming in as a novice, you may see them as all-powerful, but in truth they may not be able to see what *you* see. So keep on

> *And as you, in turn, help others to fulfill their own visions, you influence the world positively, moving it closer to an ethos built of cooperation rather than competition.*

moving, and don't stop to chat a second time. More importantly, this kind of interaction is a reminder to stick to your strategy, stay true to your dream, and to continue to embrace it and yourself, no matter what anyone else says. That unconditional embrace builds your strength.

Within six weeks of my being hired at the bank, thanks to my expedience, and perhaps especially due to strategic volunteerism— offering my help and skill wherever I could—I was promoted to head teller. Within six months, I was promoted to customer service. My bosses thought this was quite the big deal, but I had my eyes on something bigger. Unbeknownst to them, I made them my accountability partners as I continued to enhance my skills and excel in the company; every time I went in for my review and raise, I'd ask about my next step. Of course they didn't want to lose me—I'd become too valuable. But they couldn't just ignore my questions. I used their road map, however reluctantly offered, to reach my goal.

My vision was to become Vice President. When it came, almost eight years after I joined the bank, I knew it was coming. I had been working toward it all the time, nurturing the goal slowly to fruition. Because I stuck to my strategy, clung to it even when others were actively trying to sabotage my growth, my success came as no surprise to me.

Nobody can nurture a dream all by herself. For one thing, it means being able to *sell* that vision. By that, I mean being able to communicate it so that people can read your passion all over you. Then, you are able to convince others of the value of finding their own passion, "selling" opportunities to them through your own sphere of influence that they might never have thought of. When they witness your passion-driven actions, it will be so contagious that they will want to emulate what you're doing to either help themselves or a common cause, or perhaps even both.

So nurturance requires networking, aligning yourself with others in your passion and creating a positive sphere of influence around you that will help you to achieve those goals and desires that are unique to you and valuable to others. As you expand that

> *It's so important, once you discover your dream and your purpose, to do everything in your power—as if your life depends on it—to ensure that no one takes it away from you.*

sphere, opportunities will be created for you, with you, by you. And as you, in turn, help others to fulfill their own visions, you influence the world positively, moving it closer to an ethos built of cooperation rather than competition.

When I resigned from the bank, I was determined to continue my own high-powered networking for which the bank had provided a platform when I was a Vice President and representing Bank of America. As a small entrepreneur, I was still the Remi that people knew and loved. So I took that with me, and continue to volunteer and be of service wherever I can. As a social entrepreneur, character and integrity are the hallmarks of my life.

Today, my passion and my goal are to help everyone I come into contact with who needs my coaching to discover their purposes. I not only want to help them simply discover it, but also to hold their hands through the process and let them see the value they hold within.

It's so important, once you discover your dream and your purpose, to do everything in your power—as if your life depends on it—to ensure that no one takes it away from you. Carefully, strategically guide your heart, mind and soul to nurture your dream and ensure it comes to life. No one else can do it for you. The world is waiting for you to give breath to that dream.

Born in Nigeria, Remi Duyile moved to the United States in 1982, where she went on to obtain her first degree and also an MBA. While in college, Remi joined Bank of America as a teller, ultimately attaining the position of Vice President in the Retail Banking, Mortgage Banking and Premier Banking divisions. She won many awards and presided over financial portfolios for high net worth companies and individuals in Bank of America—a relationship she maintains with these premier clients. After seventeen successful years with the Bank, Remi left her position as Vice President to launch several successful business ventures in the financial services industry, including Image Consulting Group and Legacy Premier Foundation.

Remi is a speaker, coach, trainer and consultant with a passion for excellence and integrity. She believes that business can be an influential force in uplifting the human spirit and solving social problems. She uses her extensive experience in business and finance to provide counsel and create opportunities for corporations, nations, entrepreneurs, career professionals, youth and anyone who aspires to accomplish more in her life. As a business coach, Remi consults with small and minority-owned businesses to help them turn challenges into solutions and solutions into triumphs. Remi speaks on issues relating to business and financial management, networking, leadership, community development, women and youth empowerment. Visit www.RemiDuyile.com.

CHAPTER TWO

I thought, *This is pointless and humiliating,* as I walked dejectedly across campus. *Why the hell do I keep doing this?* I had just come from my doctoral advisor's office, where the twelfth draft of my candidacy paper had been rejected. *If I can't get the candidacy completed, how am I ever going to move on to my dissertation?*

As I sat on a bench, I reflected on my past accomplishments in writing and research. *I did what he said and was more careful this time,* I lamented. *Aren't I getting better? I know I'm smart enough to do this.* It seemed to me now like all my hard work was for nothing. *Maybe,* I thought, *I can't do this after all.*

Old, negative voices began to taunt me from childhood. All of the jocks and cool kids saying things like, "Dude, you can't even shoot a *basketball.* You couldn't fight your way out of a *Doritos bag.*"

Growing up in a tough, working-class neighborhood in Houston, Texas, I was the kid that got picked on and bullied for being brainy and uncoordinated. My parents encouraged me to ignore bullies or fight back, but that wasn't me. I was sensitive and took the teasing to heart. Comments about my inability to defend myself and my lack of street smarts only caused me to withdraw and harbor anger.

While I was smart and a good student, my self-esteem was low and I lacked motivation to do really well in school. Yet people encouraged me and extolled my potential and my natural abilities. My drive was most tested in my long journey with martial arts (Japanese Jujitsu in particular) and the pursuit of my doctorate.

At the advice of my boss—I was teaching at a community college at the time—I applied to the University of Houston's doctoral program in education. While everyone seemed to think I was up

> *It seemed to me now like all my hard work was for nothing.* Maybe, *I thought,* I can't do this after all.

to the task, I had no idea I was in for one of the most difficult and trying experiences of my life. Getting my doctorate, and becoming "Dr. Griggs," became my first deeply cherished dream.

I completed much of my coursework without superhuman effort. I was really enjoying school. But as time went on, I procrastinated when it came to working on my candidacy paper. I was putting lots of time and effort into helping my dojo grow, and spent many hours practicing martial arts there in the evenings. The practice helped me feel calm and grounded. I also had a full-time position at another university. My girlfriend and I had a nice life together and everything was calm and fun. Life seemed to be great.

In 2004, I met with my advisor and showed him my first draft of the first chapter of my candidacy paper. I had a strong background in liberal arts, so I was very confident in my writing skills. "It's very nice," Dr. Nora said. He pulled out four or five highlighter pens of different colors and began hacking apart the manuscript. "If I wanted leisure reading, I would read this. But I want social science. This is crap—but it's good crap." He giggled and kindly said, "I need a specific subject."

It took me five or six drafts simply to settle on a subject for the candidacy paper. And then I wrote numerous drafts. Dr. Nora was a great advisor; he helped me laugh at myself, and kept on encouraging me to be the best I could be. I was certainly thankful for that, because by the tenth and eleventh drafts the rejection really started to hurt. *Am I really good enough? Am I really smart enough?* By then, my girlfriend and I had married, and we had a little boy. There was a little tension at home, too. But I kept fighting through the self-doubt. Jujitsu helped keep me patient and focused as I recited the old samurai saying, "Fall down seven times, get up eight." Being in Japanese Jujitsu saved my life before—I knew it could help me succeed now.

After the eleventh draft, I gave even more to the twelfth than I thought I had in me. I left the twelfth draft with Dr. Nora and met with him in his office a week later, only to find out it too had been rejected. "The writing is better," he said. "But it's still disconnected. Keep working." But how? And what was the point? Sitting on my bench, I understood why some of my classmates couldn't take the demands and pressure and simply quit the program.

> Jujitsu helped keep me patient and focused as I recited the old samurai saying, "Fall down seven times, get up eight." Being in Japanese Jujitsu saved my life before—I knew it could help me succeed now.

Desolate, I sent Dr. Nora an email saying I was taking a two-month break. It was wonderful to have more time at home even though the frustration with writing made me feel isolated. One evening at the dojo, some of the students who were training for their black-belt test were getting discouraged and frustrated. I had been there once myself. I remembered my teacher, Shihan Torey Overstreet, telling us that quitting, like winning, is a habit; the only difference is that quitting is easy, but the consequences last a lifetime.

I remembered training to earn my black belt ranking. When I had earned it, I felt different. I even carried myself differently afterward. In Japanese Jujitsu, one of the primary principles is yielding. When someone pushes you, you yield to redirect the energy. This gives you the opportunity to calmly assess your situation, and time to think and use strategy rather than succumbing to your emotions.

So I changed my attitude. I redirected my energy by overriding all those naysayer-voices and re-committing to my dream: *I will be Dr. Griggs.* And I got back to work. After I submitted the seventeenth draft of Chapter One, I went to see Dr. Nora and discovered that he was in the process of moving his entire office. After helping him move I said, "Well, Dr. Nora, I've got to go. We'll reschedule to talk about the draft?" He looked up from vacuuming his new office. "Oh!" he cried, still vacuuming. "It looks good. You can move on to Chapter Two now."

Now, you may think that a grown man with a long history of martial arts training is pretty tough. I thanked Dr. Nora, and as I walked away, I couldn't hold back the tears. Finally, after almost two years and endless frustration, I could move on to Chapter Two. I walked away smiling and weeping, thinking of something Shihan Torey always used to tell us: "You know what a black belt really is? A white belt that never quits." The funny thing was, once I moved on to Chapter Two, I knew I could become Dr. Griggs.

It took almost six years, but in spring of 2010, I finally finished it. I had a supportive audience for my defense: my parents, a cousin, Shihan Torey and Anh Lee, who worked at the dojo. Due to the severe problems we were having at the time, my wife did not attend. I gave the final defense of my dissertation and waited patiently as the committee deliberated behind closed doors. The door opened, and we were all invited in again. Then my chair said, "Congratulations, Dr. Griggs." I felt like I was walking on the clouds.

On graduation day, I was giddy with happiness—we all were; some of the undergrads were break-dancing on stage when their names were called. Not one person I started my doctoral journey with, however, was walking with me. Some had graduated earlier, and some had not made it. It had been such a long road. For all my triumph and elation, I also wanted to observe the milestone with reverence, and solitary appreciation. I told my mom, dad and brother I'd walk the two and a half miles home afterward on my own.

I walked through a very tough neighborhood with a giant grin on my face—people didn't know what to make of it. It rained a little, but I walked. And I realized that I was walking from a beginning to an end. I was full of hope for the future, but I also felt a great deal of sadness, because I knew I was walking home to what would

> *Every year is a formative year, if you let it be so. And everything you learn adds to your body of knowledge and makes you a better person if you let it.*

soon be an empty house. I was resolved to grow beyond my losses and achieve even greater gains in my new life; both my doctoral journey and my marriage were done, but as some journeys end, others begin. I was going to start a new life as Dr. Griggs, and I had a beautiful little boy in my life to keep me inspired.

Your dream is attainable. You're going to have to fight for it, but fighting isn't about violence; often the real difficulty is in going through the changes it takes to get there. Change isn't always easy, but it's worth it. You're worth it. And so many others are going to benefit from your work, *if* you work. The rewards are far greater than the effort. Japanese Jujitsu taught me that you must do absolutely everything you can do with patience and focus. There is beauty in all things—and lessons to be learned, if you're willing. When you have the patience and humility to be a lifelong student, you have the potential to become a great teacher.

Every year is a formative year, if you let it be so. And everything you learn adds to your body of knowledge and makes you a better person if you let it. Getting the doctorate was one thing. Having the humility to be thankful for the whole process and the many people who helped me through it is another. It was a long road to my chapter two, but I just knew if I could sustain my effort, it would be a testament to my character and I could finally silence the voices that said, *I'm not good enough.*

Going the distance was a lesson learned—a lesson I can pass on to other people. If I had given up, how could I encourage the students at the dojo to pursue their own dreams, academic and otherwise? Now, when my son gets older and is having a bad day, I can say to him with conviction, "Son, let me tell you about the hard times your daddy had."

Keep going. Keep learning. You never know how close you are to finishing. When you serve your dream faithfully by giving it your all and never giving up, it will never stop serving you in return.

Nguyen "Tom" Griggs is a writer, researcher, life enrichment student and professional speaker. He holds an MBA in international business and finance and an EdD in higher-education administration and supervision. Sensei Tom is also a certified third-degree black belt in Japanese Jujitsu and a martial-arts instructor at TNT Jujitsu in Houston, Texas. Connect with Tom at www.TNTJujitsu.com and www. NTGriggs.com.

Cheryl L. Nicks

COMING FULL CIRCLE

In the Lower Ninth Ward of New Orleans, Louisiana, schools have still not reopened post-hurricane-Katrina. There is only one hospital here, no grocery stores and only one gas station. In fact, the area had been designated an uninhabited "Green Space" by the powers that be. It's like the Forgotten Land. But some families are fighting to bring it back. Some of us are still fighting to come home.

I travel around the city, speaking to the children of New Orleans about their health and their history, inspiring them to take a path of hope. Listening to them is even more important than speaking. I ask them: "What do you want? What do you need from us, the adults in your lives and in your community?"

One day, when I asked these questions, a little girl, about nine years old, raised her hand. In a small, determined voice, she said, "We want you all to protect us."

Looking at this little girl's earnest expression, hearing her need, I felt such deep sadness. She was living in fear in her own community. Since Hurricane Katrina, New Orleans has seen a spike in turf and drug wars, economic depression and violence among young males. Too often, the kids see reports of shootings and violence on the news. How could I help show the youth of our community a different path? How could I help them to understand that their environment does not define who they are?

When I was a young girl growing up in New Orleans, I loved to play with the kids in the neighborhood—especially the boys. We had fun playing marbles and touch football in the street, or in my grandmother's yard. As we got older, I watched my friends

> *How could I help show the youth of our community a different path? How could I help them to understand that their environment does not define who they are?*

progressively get into more and more trouble. They were unaware of their choices and their potential, created chaos in their homes and got into altercations at school and in the neighborhood. Some of them were living with domestic violence or alcoholism at home. Some of them were put out of school and ended up in and out of jail.

Dice games were frequent, and they usually ended in a fight and a police chase. I can remember seeing a young man dead of a drug overdose in an abandoned house, with a needle still in his arm. One day one of the boys I played with was gunned down in my grandmother's front yard. I said, *No! No! That will not be my reality. I will choose a different path!*

My four younger siblings, my mom and I lived in the Lower Ninth Ward with my maternal grandmother in a big, old two-story wooden house. My grandmother played the piano and organ for different churches. I adored her, and was always right beside her. Neither she nor my mother ever drank, smoked or partied, and they stressed the importance of education. They drew a lot of strength from their religious faith and never let hardship defeat them. Watching the way they chose to live, I was encouraged. I wanted to be like *them*. Raised by my mother and my grandmother—a pair of very strong women—I learned very early that the trajectory of my life was a matter of my own, deliberate choices.

My grandmother was the type of person who would take in all the neighborhood kids, and feed anyone who stopped by. There were always lots of people gathered at the house and lots of kids playing in the front yard. Young ladies would drop their babies off with us, sometimes for weeks at a time. From the age of ten on, as the oldest grandchild, I was always caring for babies and younger children, and I loved it.

When I was fourteen, I started volunteering at the Charity Hospital, where I (and most African-Americans in the area) had been born. The east side of the hospital was for "colored" people, and the west was for whites. On my summer breaks, I fed and read to children and babies in the east-side pediatric ward.

> *Raised by my mother and my grandmother—a pair of very strong women—I learned very early that the trajectory of my life was a matter of my own, deliberate choices.*

I saw nursing as my way out, and a way to continue to take care of people, especially babies and children. I was already working as a Licensed Practical Nurse when I applied to school to become a Registered Nurse, and was very excited to be called for an interview. The admissions counselor, however, looked at me and said that my standardized test scores were too low, and I would need to "go somewhere and take remedial math and English." My heart and spirit were crushed. But I was determined. I took the courses, applied to nursing school a second time and was accepted.

That was in the 1970s, in the South. It wasn't easy for African-Americans to get into nursing school, or anywhere else. The school had not previously admitted African-Americans, and I'd grown up in a society steeped in racism. So the racism itself was no surprise, but I was shocked when one of the nuns actually said, remorsefully, "I'm ashamed to admit that we did practice discrimination. And when we started accepting government funding, we could no longer legally discriminate." I could tell that she didn't think the discrimination was right. But most of the instructors didn't feel the way she did. Racism in school was still virulent and made getting an education very difficult. Many of our teachers tried to discourage us—some wanted to force us to give up and drop out.

Two of us were LPNs, a white woman and myself. We both tested to opt out of a class at the same time. The instructor said the test was "pretty difficult," and would take about two hours. I finished it in about an hour and fifteen minutes. We came back after lunch for our results. The instructor told the white nurse, "You passed the test." Then she turned to me and said, "You didn't pass. You needed a 77 and your score is 75." "May I see the test paper?" I asked. "Oh no, that's not allowed," she replied, with a strange little smile at the corner of her mouth.

I knew what the game was. And I thought about fighting or complaining, but knew that if I did, they would make it even harder for me and I might never finish school. I took the class that semester. The next semester I was allowed to take a test to opt out of another class, and the same thing happened. I felt dejected, but because I already knew the history and lived the discrimination, I wasn't surprised. Many times my papers came back with a big red "X" through them, with no feedback, no explanation. In class, I felt invisible. Many days and nights I cried and thought about giving up. But I suppressed my feelings and kept going, because my dream was bigger than the human obstacles.

Unfortunately, most of my fellow African–American students were bullied out of school and only six of us persevered and graduated. That day felt like a dream. I walked proudly across the stage to receive my Registered Nurse degree, knowing I had won. *You did it!* I told myself. *You did it! You are an RN! No one can ever take that away from you.* My mother was so proud of me. Only my grandmother, who had died four months earlier, was missing on that triumphant day.

For decades, now, I've continued to work with babies, children and teenagers. One day, listening to Les Brown, I was struck by something he said: "Whatever you will do for free—that is your passion." I realized that this, for me, is speaking to our youth. It is, in essence, speaking to our future.

A couple of years before Katrina, I dreamed of a youth center in the Lower Ninth. Katrina exposed the urgency of that need. Its aftermath is indeed a crisis, but also an opportunity to reclaim our community. My dream has materialized into a not-for-profit foundation whose mission is to rebuild communities around the

> *To rebuild our community, we need our youth to know they aren't victims. They have to know that they can turn their wounds into wisdom, and that their circumstances don't create their destinies, they do.*

world from the *youth* up, and to protect our children—like that nine-year-old girl who asked for help, like the little boys I talk to who remind me of the friends I used to play marbles with— by helping change mindsets in the community from negative to positive, from hopeless to hopeful. That powerful dream is calling me, drawing me back to the Lower Ninth, and I have to return. It's like I've come full circle.

Slowly, people are starting to move back to the Lower Ninth, thanks in great part to some determined residents and community leaders, and the efforts of Brad Pitt, who committed to rebuild one hundred fifty homes here even after the rebuilding of New Orleans was neglected and ignored by government agencies. He is still in the building phase; about fifty homes have been completed, and volunteers from all over the world continue to come and help with the rebuilding. Some former residents have lost too much to ever be able to rebuild their lives here, but hope is being rekindled.

To rebuild our community, we need our youth to know they aren't victims. They have to know that they can turn their wounds into wisdom, and that their circumstances don't create their destinies, *they* do. As Les Brown says, "Every child is reachable, teachable and redeemable."

> *"We have two primary choices in life, to accept conditions*
> *as they exist or take responsibility and change them."*
> —Denis Waitley

I've never left New Orleans, except to evacuate, and there are thousands like me. We're not going to let anyone tell us, or our children, that we don't belong here—we're not going to let anyone take home away.

Cheryl L. Nicks is a sought-after author, speaker and poet with a strong passion for youth empowerment. She has inspired audiences locally and nationally with her speeches and poetry. Her book, Poems for the Heart with Steps to Grow By *is available in print and on CD on Amazon.com. Cheryl has been personally coached by Mark Victor Hansen, co-author of the* Chicken Soup for the Soul *series; and by Les Brown, with whom she's also shared the stage. Her vision for the mission of the Nicks International Community Foundation is to foster community emotional wellbeing, unity and youth literacy—creating future leaders who will create healthy, safe, literate communities around the world in turn. Connect with Cheryl at www.CherylNicksEnterprises. com and www.NicksFoundation.org.*

Ming Wong

TAMING THE TIGERS

There is an old Chinese proverb:

明知山有虎，
偏向虎山行。

Knowing that there is a tiger residing in the mountain,
I still dare venture into it.

The tiger is a symbol of the fears we wrestle with. I love this old proverb because it reminds us that courage is not the absence of fear, but the willingness to confront it and persevere.

I was born in China. The day my mother decided to leave my father and walk away from their marriage was the day she discovered that she was pregnant with me. My mother and father divorced soon after I came into the world, and both left me by the time I was two. I grew up with my grandfather, who worked a lot and was rarely around, and Seipoa, a wise older lady who had worked for my grandfather's family for many years.

Abandoned by my parents, I always knew and felt that I was different. Everyone else had two parents—the only single parents were widows and widowers—and no one even spoke the word "divorce." Having no parents at all was almost like being illegitimate. I wished I could have said that my parents were dead, but everyone knew they'd left me. My friends and classmates taunted me until I finally started making up stories: "My parents love me, they're just far away. They're coming to visit me soon." But they never did. As I got older and they still failed to come for me, I felt more and more worthless.

I was completely alone—except for Seipoa, my guardian angel. When I was fifteen, she came to me and said, "Ming, you have to be independent. Your grandfather and I are getting old, and we will not be able to care for you much longer." Seipoa counseled me to enter nursing school. "Nursing is a career you can always count on. And if you rise to this challenge, especially at your age, you will finally know deep inside that you are better than an

> *Knowing that there is a tiger residing in the mountain, I still dare venture into it.*

unwanted child." Facing my first tiger, she told me, I would begin to build a foundation of strength within. "It will not be easy," she said, "but I know you can do it. This is your way to freedom." She was right.

A short while later, I entered the tiger's mouth: three years of intensive study far from home and Seipoa, the only one who believed I could handle the hard work and demanding class-load. The hospital was cold, dark and forbidding; at first I was terrified of the sick and dying. I worked and took classes every day but Sunday, when I was allowed a short leave from campus. I was so exhausted by the long hours of work that I often thought I wouldn't make it. But then I'd take a deep breath and listen to a voice inside me say, *You are going to be all right, just keep going.*

I began to work on making my body physically healthy and strong. At first it was to withstand the rigors of school, but after a while I noticed a change happening in my mind. As my body became more vibrant, my thoughts did too. One day, sitting outside, I experienced my first moment of pure self-acceptance. I realized, "I have a lot to be proud of." Maybe being unwanted by my parents had served me. Maybe it wasn't my fault that they left.

I'm not so bad—if I can face this extreme challenge, what could I do next?

After I tamed my first tiger, the rest became progressively easier to face. I graduated and moved to another city, where I realized my dream of becoming fully independent: I found a job in a hospital and worked as a private nurse on the weekends, too, keeping my body strong and flexible so I didn't strain myself or become overtired.

During this time, I visited my parents. They were both remarried, with new families and new children. Ashamed of their divorce, neither of them introduced me as their daughter. Instead, they called me their "god-daughter." This really hurt, but it didn't shatter me.

Working two and sometimes three jobs, I saved a substantial amount of money. So, when I was presented with the opportunity to come to America, I jumped at it. Upon arrival, however, I faced another snarling tiger: not being able to speak English. To

> *Each tiger I faced and tamed proved to me that I could create the reality that I wanted to live in.*

be fully independent, I needed to learn how to drive. But with no English, how could I take the driver's test? Knowing myself, now, as someone with patience and stamina, I took the handbook home and worked one word and then one sentence at a time, using my dictionary to translate them into Chinese. I worked at this every day for three months, passing the exam on my first try.

Each tiger I faced and tamed proved to me that I *could* create the reality that I wanted to live in. Due to my past experiences of facing my tigers, I was able to use the courage and strength I gained to start a new business with my husband while raising two small children. I started practicing Tai Chi, and found that the discipline continued to unlock places in my mind where I still struggled with trauma and resulting low self-esteem. So when I discovered Pilates, which I loved, it was not so scary to become an instructor. It was exciting. The only place I really remained stuck was feeling self-conscious about my accent.

To be true to yourself, to truly fight for your dreams, self-acceptance is key. When I found that my accent resonated with many people, and actually helped me reach them, I embraced it—and myself as a public speaker. I came to terms with the fact that my accent is not a weakness; rather, it is another strength, as it makes me different from the dominant culture.

Being an unwanted child also appeared to others as a weakness—it certainly did to me, for a long time. But in the end, it was part of my strength. I think Seipoa knew that. Uniqueness is a strength that sets each of us apart from each other. It is the beauty that we see in ourselves whenever we look in the mirror. I am someone to me, first.

Now, after each time I speak, I listen to immigrant men and women talk about their own accents and how they've been afraid to stand up and speak in a public forum. Listening to me brings them hope and shows them that if I can do it, they can do it too.

I'm not perfect, but I'm still out there speaking. You don't have to be perfect either. You only have to be yourself. Maybe the tiger that blocks us from embracing that knowledge is the most frightening one of all.

Life can look dark. Material wealth disappears in an instant. Loved ones get sick. We make decisions we regret. But if you look deep inside and see what you can trust yourself to bring to the table under any circumstances, be assured that you *will* come through. It doesn't matter where you started from—you can create the reality you want.

Identify the tiger in the mountain by standing up for yourself, especially in times when you feel abandoned. Accept who you are when you decide to meet that tiger! This means embracing both your strengths and your weaknesses. You are whole. You *can* take action and face your first tiger! It is more than worthwhile to do it—entering the tiger's mouth is always the first step toward your ultimate dream.

Remember to breathe whenever you face a tiger. After twenty-plus years doing Tai Chi, and in my work helping people balance body and mind, I know that the two are connected only when we're consciously breathing! You need to be grounded to face the tiger, which also means working on your physical and emotional

> It doesn't matter where you started from—you can create the reality you want.

health. The body is a projection of the mind, and your body will *feed* your mind as you dance with your tigers. Affirm yourself as much as you can, and treat yourself well by putting yourself first. And celebrate your victories over your tigers! If you don't do this, no one will.

It has taken plenty of time and attention to work from within to understand the deep hurt of my childhood, and know how to deal with it. Occasionally that tiger still sneaks up on me and triggers strong emotional reactions and intense vulnerability. I have to be really aware, speaking gently to myself as a caring parent might to a frightened little girl: *Ming, it's going to be okay. You're all grown up and strong now.* Self-talk helps me a lot! Know your tigers, and all their tricks. Then be gentle with yourself if you fall for them.

Don't give up—continue to face the tigers in your life. In fact, make a point of pursuing them. For each one you face has a greater gift of self-awareness to offer you, and each will be easier to conquer than the last. Your courage will be rewarded with big dreams fulfilled.

What is holding you back in your own journey to the mountain? What kind of tigers are you facing in your life today? I cannot know your story, but I do know that when you face your tigers, understand them, even make friends with them, you will overcome them. And when you tame those tigers, you will discover who you really are. No tiger can steal your essence away.

Ming Wong specializes in strengthening the core of the human spirit and the structure of the human frame by aligning the body with the mind. She blends Eastern and Western philosophies, enabling her clients to realign their lives by strengthening their bodies. As a certified Pilates instructor and wellness professional, Ming continually collaborates with physicians, physical therapists and chiropractors to better serve her clients. Having studied under many masters, she has developed a unique holistic approach to healing by using a variety of modalities. She is also a respected Tai Chi practitioner of over twenty years. As an inspirational speaker, Ming has trained with Les Brown, her mentor. She also holds a seat in his Platinum Speakers Program. As an entrepreneur, Ming, along with her husband and two children, has run a successful family business in Southern California for over twenty years. Connect with Ming at www.MingSpeaks.com.

Dr. Ramesh Kumar

MY DRIVING FORCE

My dream began with a nightmare. In 1977, I was eighteen and living with my family in a modest house in Bangalore, India. We were lower middle class. Years before, my father had declared bankruptcy, having had a string of business failures; shortly after that, he died, leaving my mother, my three siblings and me in the lurch. Rayappa came to our rescue. Rayappa was my brother-in-law, married to my second sister, Parvati. But he was also my mentor and my family's savior. He made a meager salary as a government clerk, but with that money he fed my mother, me, two of my brothers, my sister and their two-year-old son. Whatever we needed, he helped provide, and oftentimes that included sound advice.

In 1977, Rayappa was diagnosed with testicular cancer. He underwent surgery, but the prognosis wasn't good. The cancer had spread, and he was given just a few months to live—but he was determined to fight as long as he could, and I was determined to help him. For several weeks, I drove him to his daily radiation treatments at a cancer clinic in Bangalore. Rayappa was losing weight so rapidly that, on our scooter, he looked like a mere skeleton of a man, his arms thin as ropes wrapped around my waist, hanging on. I was in college, and I wanted to drop out and get a job, but he told me I couldn't.

At the clinic, he disappeared into a maze of corridors to receive his treatment, and I was never allowed to follow him. Huge steel doors opened like a mouth, and he would be swallowed into this maze, the doors closing behind him, cutting me and everyone else off from all knowledge of what was happening. I inquired, but the people who worked there were mean and nasty and never answered my questions.

Likewise, the doctors were arrogant and callous; we had to bribe them just to get information about Rayappa's case. I couldn't understand why it was so difficult to get information. *Does Rayappa need medications? Does he need a new liver? Is there something we should be doing that we're not? Why won't they talk?* This was no way to treat ill people and their families. From my anger, a dream was born: I decided to become a doctor and do things differently, to do things the *right* way.

Rayappa's health continued to worsen. One night, he took Parvati, my elder brother and me out to dinner. "I don't have much longer," he said. I wept openly. "I have arranged a job for Parvati in the department where I work." My sister had never held a job before, but she was going to have to now. "She will use the money to support the family, and she will use it to support you, Ramesh. You absolutely must finish college. You are the one in the family who is a studier; you are the one who can pull the family out of its hole."

A few weeks later, he died. I was devastated. The whole ordeal had been the worst months of my life, and now that he was dead, I wanted only to quit school, get a job and support my family. But my family wouldn't let me. My sister assumed her job with the government, and my older brother got a job fixing cars at a small workshop. They gave me money to help me buy books and pay my way through medical school. My mother sold family jewelry that had been handed down through generations and gave me money for clothes. They were all sacrificing for me, and I couldn't let them down.

All I did was study—non-stop. I could not let my family down. And my brother-in-law was a driving force. When I studied, I thought of him, and I studied all of the time. I had nothing else to do. I had my books, and I had time, so I had all I needed. My dream was to be a doctor, and I was using my time to fulfill that dream. Whatever your dream is, you have twenty-four hours a day to make it a reality, so use them all. Time is one of the basic necessities to achieve dreams, so if you're wasting time, you're wasting your dream.

And so I continued studying diligently, studying harder than everyone else around me. Achieving your dream often comes down to how badly you want it. And how badly you want something is expressed through action, not words or mere desire. There was a

> *Whatever your dream is, you have twenty-four hours a day to make it a reality, so use them all. Time is one of the basic necessities to achieve dreams, so if you're wasting time, you're wasting your dream.*

time in my life when I turned only five percent of my thoughts and desires into action, and during that time I achieved nothing. But when I turned eighty percent of my thoughts into action, the benefits started to accrue and continue to do so today.

I finally graduated medical school, and I did so with little fanfare. In America, people celebrate degrees and graduations with major parties, but it was not like that for me. The attitude was much more restrained: "You earned your degree, you deserved it, now go find a job." I did find a job—at a clinic where I was paid ten dollars a month. That was absolute heaven. I also found a wife.

I married an incredibly wonderful woman whom I met in Bangalore, a person who shared my goals and philosophy. And in 1987, I made my way to the United States. I was told by several of my friends and colleagues, "It's really tough to get into residency training in the United States at this time. Several people like you who immigrated to the States, were unable to get into training and are currently working as gas station attendants and janitors." This encouraged me to try even harder to achieve my dreams!

To be a doctor in America, I had to have some more education. I passed my entrance exams with flying colors and got accepted to the Internal Medicine Program at Wayne State University. My scores were so incredibly good that the program director offered me the position based on just a five-minute phone interview and made sure that I sent in a signed contract within a couple of days. I don't mention my scores to brag. I didn't have much time to study for these tests. But because I had studied so hard years before, I had given myself such a strong educational foundation. Again, the lesson: use what time you have to its utmost now, because you never know what time you won't have in the future.

> *I was tormented by the idea of reliving those days in India when I had to take my brother-in-law for his radiation treatments. To train in radiation would mean emotionally going through all of that again.*

I decided to become a cardiologist. While finishing my cardiology internship, I happened to walk by the radiation department of the university. I felt a strong urge to go inside and ask for a training position to become a radiation oncologist, but I resisted it for several days.

I was tormented by the idea of reliving those days in India when I had to take my brother-in-law for his radiation treatments. To train in radiation would mean emotionally going through all of that again. What's more, when I bounced the idea off my friends, they all said that it was impossible to get a training position in such a high-tech field as radiation oncology. This was in 1989, back when radiation was still a very secretive world—a milieu of basement medicine and introverted doctors.

But I couldn't resist my curiosity; I had to know all about the technology that was used to help cancer patients. More importantly, I couldn't resist my heart. Everyone around me was saying "no," but my heart was saying "yes," and so was my wife. We had many conversations about what I should do, and she kept saying, "Ramesh, do what you think is right." So I did. I went by the Radiation Oncology Department, stepped into the lobby and handed my resumé to the receptionist. Less than half an hour later I got a phone call from the program director, telling me that she was so impressed with my resumé that she promised to create a position for me through a special request of the university.

And so I began studying to be a radiation oncologist. The training was heartrending, because it brought an onslaught of memories that were still incredibly hard for me to endure. But my

> *Once you build a strong vision of where you want to go, you have to fortify it with a strong reason for it.*

program director took very special care of me. She knew what I'd gone through, and she helped me cope during the difficult times. I often had half a mind to dump everything and head back into cardiology, but she'd say to me, "Hang in there, Ramesh. You're the best we have."

And I did hang in there, because I had a new dream: I wanted to help as many cancer patients as I could, and in a way that was completely unlike my brother-in-law's experience. I wanted cancer patients to have a friendly, open, loving, nurturing experience with their doctors. I wanted their families to be included in the process so that they could feel cared for, too. These desires were paramount to my dream.

Once you build a strong vision of where you want to go, you have to fortify it with a strong reason for it. In other words, once you establish the "what" of your dream, you have to establish the "why," and if your why is weak, it will either not sustain you through the difficult times, or at the least it will slow down the process of achieving your dreams. I became a radiation oncologist, and in my work I have achieved the material success I'd always hoped for plus personal gratification from helping so many people. In fact, it is the helping that gives me the energy to keep going 24/7. There have been mistakes and failures. But the first thing I do after a failure is to look back, analyze what I did wrong, and glean some life lessons to make sure I don't repeat those mistakes.

My dream is like a movie script with no ending, an ever-evolving saga with new chapters being added every day. The core of what I do continues to expand and evolve toward new ways to cure patients. I want to build a bridge between traditional medicine, such as chemotherapy and radiation, and complementary medicine, such as yoga and meditation.

Several families have stories similar to Rayappa's, and some of them have come through the doors of my practice. I know I make a huge difference in their lives as I take care that none endure the agony I experienced. Maybe I will inspire the next generation of Dr. Kumars to carry on the work and the philosophy of taking care of cancer patients in a way that they crave and deserve.

My new area of interest is to teach and mentor physicians regarding managing their businesses. Many doctors are incredible when it comes to medicine, but they're of no use to anyone if they can't pay their light bills. Am I working hard? Absolutely. Am I sacrificing? Sure. But relatively speaking, my sacrifice is only a fraction of the sacrifice Rayappa endured making for my family and me. And I am mindful that every patient I treat may well be the Rayappa of some other family, who needs its Rayappa as much as I needed mine. That's why I treat every patient as if I'm treating Rayappa, the driving force behind everything I do.

Born in Bangalore, India, Dr. Ramesh Kumar was raised in a business family but turned his sights to medicine at an early age. He completed medical school in India, and then moved to the United States, where he studied to become a radiation oncologist. In 1994, he established Coastal CyberKnife (www.CoastalCyberKnife.com), a private practice that has revolutionized cancer care. His clinic is a state-of-the-art facility with the best-trained staff and support system, and his style of practice is holistic, catering to the physical and emotional needs of both patient and family. Learn more about Ramesh at www.CuringCancerOfTheMind.com.

Rosemary McDowell

AS YOU FLY

My dream was always to be a writer. I believe I discovered that at about age twelve, when I sat down and wrote a script for one of my favorite TV shows, *Bonanza,* on spec. I wrote it in secret, while pretending to do my homework. If my parents had found out, they would have told me it was a waste of time. The first draft I wrote longhand—then I typed it up with a few minor changes on my first typewriter according to submission guidelines. I found just the right envelope, walked it to the post office, mailed it, and waited. Of course it was rejected, but that didn't make me want to stop.

I didn't form a vision for my life as a writer, because at home I was always being told I needed to go to college and major in business so I could get a good job. I'm a native of Washington, D.C., where everybody ends up working for the government. There was a lot of pressure on me to do the same. Boy, did my family love it when I majored in linguistics. I did it in protest, but mostly I did it for myself.

I knew I wanted to write in college, but I also knew I needed to be away from home. So even though I couldn't take only writing classes at Georgetown, I chose courses that required plenty of writing, and professors who put lots of essay questions on their tests, instead of boring multiple choice questions. I had fun writing the essays. It hardly mattered what kind of writing I was doing, as long as I was doing it.

Because I wanted to be independent, I took the first job I could find (a full time summer job at the White House—government after all), and then it was just going from one job to the next, knowing I wanted to write but not having the slightest idea how to make it pay. I realized that I needed a measure of financial freedom, and that I would find ways to write in my jobs, just as I'd done in college.

Back in the 60s and 70s, most women were just beginning to establish their working lives. The expectation was still get married, have kids. To work full-time and not be financially dependent on my husband was good for my soul, and it came in handy once our

> *After an ugly divorce, I was a single parent. I couldn't just toss away my government job and write the great American novel—I had to find a way to make my dream work for all concerned.*

marriage revealed itself to be a lot like *The War of the Roses*. I felt like I was fighting all the stereotypes. My mother used to hang up on my secretary when he answered the phone, because he was a man.

After an ugly divorce, I was a single parent. I couldn't just toss away my government job and write the great American novel—I had to find a way to make my dream work for all concerned. So I bounced from career to career in the government, always looking for my niche. To pay the bills, I had several government jobs in accounting, facilities management and information technology. But these careers didn't do it for me. When I found contracting, which involved writing and reviewing others' writing, I got pretty excited.

But working for the government was not my cup of tea. Things could drag on and on for years and never change. No one seemed to get anything done, but neither were they ever fired. I had a secretary who kept booze in the bottom drawer of her filing cabinet, just like in an old black-and-white detective movie. It took me three years to get her fired. "Help me get her out of here," I said to Human Resources. "She's boozing it up in the office."

I got a memo weeks later: "We've got to at least give her a chance."

"A chance?" I wrote. "She's so drunk she can't even answer the phone!" That's the way it tended to go.

Finally, I just had to step out on a ledge and out of my comfort zone. I had to face it: I hated government work. For someone with

> *Before, it was all about the have-tos. I can't this, because I have to do that. Now I just think about the want-tos. I enjoy saying: I am a writer.*

real curiosity, it was drudgery. Moving through all those different agencies, I had never found a place where I could work the way I wanted to work. I had already put in sixteen years—there was no way I could face another nineteen years just to collect that now-extinct creature, the healthy civil service pension. People told me I was crazy to leave that kind of security, but I thought that doing what I really wanted to do was freedom, and that freedom was real security.

I would have been so unhappy if I'd stayed. And if you're unhappy with yourself, you can't move ahead. I still wanted to write. And I knew I couldn't play by their rules anymore. So one day, I just up and quit. That was my first big step, but there were plenty of little ones behind me that weren't apparent until much later in my life.

I spent the next ten years working in private industry. The best thing about that, by far, was the proposal writing. I loved it. I would catch myself saying out loud, "Look! I'm writing!" It took me twenty years, after I left college, to do anything like what I considered "real" writing, and I enjoyed it so much. I became an expert at writing contracts and proposals that made millions for the companies I was working for, but barely even got me a pat on the back.

Finally, I had had it with working for other people, and I started my own business helping small businesses with their proposals and contracts.

One of the reasons I've always loved writing so much is that any piece of writing has a beginning, a middle and an end. A proposal, like a story, needs to stand out. It needs to have a certain something that makes it shine. In the midst of the unavoidable dry data, something has to pique interest. If you've told your story, and highlighted something unique, you've done your job. Once you're done, you're done—no government purgatory necessary. Can you tell I love my job?

I really enjoy sitting down and writing a business plan or a contract, putting all those pieces together and seeing a final product emerge, its ends tied up like a story with a happy ending.

> *I never gave up on my dream, even if I didn't get to it as the crow flies. Very few of us, actually, fly in a straight line.*

But the best thing by far is to be able to write full time. It feels like total freedom. I don't need anybody telling me yes or no. I can simply tell myself *yes*.

Before, it was all about the have-tos. I can't this, because I have to do that. Now I just think about the want-tos. I enjoy saying: I am a writer. It's a new direction. I have financial freedom. I'm taking the summer off for the first time ever. I get to conduct business ethically without struggling with anybody else about it. For the first time, I don't feel stressed. I'm comfortable. That's saying a lot, because that list of have-tos always stressed me out.

For a while now, I have wanted to write how-to books about proposal and grant-writing, simple, down-to-earth volumes with type you can read and spaces in the margins to make notes in. But there was always some reason I didn't have time. I'm glad I never forgot that dream, and never threw away my notes and outlines. I've been working toward this for a long time. Now I've made the space to follow through.

The route to my dream wasn't your garden-variety Rocky Balboa journey. It took me through plenty of twists and turns, weaving through a whole crazy maze of occupations. But none of them was a waste of my time: my twists and turns built my career. It may not be *Bonanza,* but it's good for me. I never gave up on my dream, even if I didn't get to it as the crow flies. Very few of us, actually, fly in a straight line.

I always knew I would get here, I just didn't know how, or exactly what it would look like. That's nothing to be afraid of. Don't get stuck thinking you need to drop everything in order to pursue a single path to your dream. Life isn't really like that. It's not always even possible.

Start where you are, with your family obligations or expectations, your issues of not feeling strong enough, confident enough, or needing further education. If you need to start by pulling yourself through a long series of tough circumstances before a big opportunity presents itself, then you'll be all the stronger when you meet the dream that waits for you. You may need to meander a long time to find where you need to be.

But don't give up! Too many people get discouraged by the changes and challenges and quit too soon, when their dream is just around the bend. Persevere just a little longer, take that extra step, wait that extra week. Even if your job isn't exactly the right one according to your dream-picture, it may be leading you to exactly where you need to go. Sometimes your steps don't look like anything individually, but when you put them all together, they add up to something big.

Anything you do in life leads you to something. All my jobs contributed to what I do now, without my realizing it when I was trudging through them. I always found ways to write, even if the circumstances didn't look glamorous. And I've always been a big reader, and made time for it. *"Novels?"* some said. Yes! That was part of keeping the light on my path. All roads lead to your dream, if you really let it stay alive inside of you.

Your dream is always out there somewhere, waiting for you. It guides you to itself, in all your life choices.

Rosemary McDowell is a full-time, working writer who is busy developing easy how-to books on government contracting and recently published her first book, Demystifying Government Contracting. *She is a CEO Space faculty member and an expert on assuring small business does not leave the largest customer on earth, the US government, out of their future client relationship plans for growth. She helps businesses grow through her unique, proven perspective on government contracting, board management and administration, and risk mitigation/workplace integrity. She is The Beltway Navigator™ The Virtual Chairwoman™ and The Corporate Risk Mitigator™. Much awarded for her accomplishments in business and service, Rosemary is a member of CEO Space, NCMA, NAWBO and Executive Women's Roundtable. She is featured in Mary Ann Halpin's book,* Fearless Women, Fearless Wisdom. *Connect with Rosemary at www.RosemaryMcDowell.com.*

Charmaine Smith, Esq.

THE ROOT IN YOU

When I was a teenager, I knew exactly what I wanted to be: a lawyer. And I knew the precise path I needed to travel to be one. But not everyone thought I had what it took. In high school, my careers advisor said, "Becoming a lawyer will cost you way too much money. You should pursue something else." Meanwhile, when the person next to me said she wanted to become a lawyer, the careers advisor told her, "Great choice. I think you can make it." The only difference between the two of us was the color of our skin.

I did not walk away from that meeting deflated or defeated. In fact, I walked away inspired to fight even harder. I knew I had what it took to be a lawyer. My family had the money necessary to support me. And I had an older cousin who had passed the New York State bar and was a prosecuting attorney there. If I couldn't make it in England, I would make it somewhere else. I would be a lawyer, and I was determined not to let others' perception of me become my reality.

I had other allies, too. My teachers knew my potential and knew what I wanted, so they made it possible for me to work in a solicitor's firm. And I had my family, whose support has always been undeviating and undying. Most important, I had God. We must have faith to work a dream, and God is always there to help us. God knows what is needed to move us to the next level. Don't worry about what you do not have. God always makes up the difference. Work with what God has provided and the rest will follow. Philippians 1:6: "He who began a good work in you will carry it on to completion."

So in 1997, I began to study for my law degree. I worked very hard, determined to graduate in 2000, but another obstacle entered my path. I got pregnant, and three months after my daughter was born, we learned she had sickle cell anemia, an inherited blood disorder whose symptoms can be crippling. I now needed to find a way to be able to dedicate my life to my daughter *and* my studies.

Once again, I turned to my faith for guidance and support. The Apostle Paul famously tells us that, "Faith without works is dead." I absorbed that teaching. In order for me to continue my studies, continue my path, I had to have faith that my daughter was going to be okay. If I didn't believe that, my entire mindset would have changed, and that could have led me somewhere else entirely.

But belief is not enough; you have to work on that belief. And so I worked that much harder after she was born—I was ready. My own mother had always told me that where there's a will, there's a way, and she'd always raised us to work twice as hard as everyone else. So I didn't buckle under the pressure. I greeted it, embraced it, worked twice as hard under it, and in June 2001, I graduated with an LLB law degree with honors. Pressure makes diamonds; the more the pressure, the more beautiful the diamond.

I momentarily put my studies on hold in order to take care of my daughter, and when I resumed school, I decided to become a solicitor rather than a barrister. I embarked on a part-time legal practice course that would allow me to look after my daughter full-time, but still provide me with a postgraduate law diploma. I studied part time for two years, and in December 2003, I graduated. The next step was to secure a training contract, but I got pregnant again, and once more all my plans went out the window.

Life now took a different course. I was faced with the prospect of a second child with sickle cell anemia. We were tested during the pregnancy, and by the grace of God everything was clear, but I became preoccupied with the idea of helping other people in similar situations. So I took part in studies, and I worked with the Sickle Cell and Thalassemia Society, helping with press briefings and encouraging parents to get tested for sickle cell and thalassemia traits.

But something else was happening with me. My dreams were changing. Being a solicitor was no longer a priority. Helping others was. And yet, to be able to help others, the knowledge and skills I acquired while studying law were going to be invaluable. In other words, I was always on the path, but the final destination was

> Pressure makes diamonds; the more the pressure, the more beautiful the diamond.

starting to appear as if it might be located somewhere other than where I'd first imagined. And my path was changing because of challenges that had come my way. But I learned that there are no challenges in life, just experiences that will lead to your destiny.

So what was my destiny now? I needed to find out. I needed to reevaluate my priorities and dreams. I had to ask the key questions: What do I want from my life? How do I get there? And what am I willing to do to make it happen? Looking deep within, I answered the first question. My children taught me so much, and in slowing down and caring for them, I realized what was worth fighting for: children and young people.

Fighting for your dreams is having the vision, beyond your current circumstances, to achieve what you have set your mind on. I'd set my mind on a life of helping young people, so now it was time to decide how to get there. I became a volunteer for families in dire circumstances. I worked as a legal advisor in housing, and I helped children who were getting evicted.

I also worked directly with children, mentoring them. I volunteered for a mentoring program, and I worked mostly with gang members or young people who were in jail. This is an incredibly difficult population to work with, because the odds they must overcome to change their lives are enormous. But I wouldn't work with them if I didn't think those odds could be overcome, and if I couldn't be the one to help them do it.

Believe. Have faith that something positive will happen, and those thoughts you had in the back of your mind will come to fruition. As the Bible says, in Matthew 17:20, if you have faith like a mustard seed, nothing will be impossible to you.

When I worked with these young people, I asked them what they wanted to do with their lives. When they told me, I asked, "How do you want to achieve that?" They were silent. They simply didn't know how to make that transformation. So I guided them. I encouraged them to read in order to develop their minds. I

> *Believe. Have faith that something positive will happen, and those thoughts you had in the back of your mind will come to fruition. As the Bible says, in Matthew 17:20, if you have faith like a mustard seed, nothing will be impossible to you.*

also offered them new experiences—somewhere different to go, something different to do. That not only broadened their perceptions and understandings, it also opened their minds to further new experiences.

I also asked them, "In jail, who were your friends?" When they told me, I asked, "If you told these friends your new plans, would they help?" Most of the time, they said, "No." And that's key. When you are fighting for your dreams, it's vital to surround yourself with people who have a positive mindset, people who believe in your dreams, people who are interested in assisting and not obstructing.

I was so successful in helping some of these youths that I was approached more and more to help others. My dream widened, and my passion became to encourage others to move beyond their present circumstances. I redoubled my efforts to do precisely that. I enrolled in various necessary courses, and I also became incorporated into a multi-level marketing plan that encouraged successful thinking. Again, the dream kept altering, but I continued to roll with the changes. When opportunity offers its hand, don't second guess it. Simply take it within your own hand and walk in faith. Who knows where it will lead?

The only way to end up further along tomorrow than where we are today is to increase our exposure and open our minds. We move along the path of life only as we experience new things, think new

> *Again, the dream kept altering, but I continued to roll with the changes. When opportunity offers its hand, don't second guess it. Simply take it within your own hand and walk in faith. Who knows where it will lead?*

thoughts, entertain new ideas, meet new people, see new visions, dream new dreams, take new risks and recognize new potential. You need exposure to develop a broad mind.

And yet, for all of the changes on my path, one basic element has never changed, and that is the root in me. Many years ago, I thought the root in me was to practice law; but knowledge of the law, I later realized, was just a tool I needed. The root in me was actually my passion for helping others. As you grow and gain in knowledge and experience, your vision changes, but the root in you is always the same. You just need to find out what the root in you is, or at least be open to learning it at some point in your journey.

We can all make our dreams come true if we just believe the impossible is possible—and then fight to make the impossible possible. I believe dreams can come true if we step out from the darkness into the light, and greet challenges as mere stepping-stones to the future. You have to believe, but you have to work on that belief, too.

So move forward, but have patience. God promises to bless you, so don't give up too soon. Life is all about the blessings you will receive and the challenges you will face. When times are tough, rely on the silent force within, and when times are good, smile wide and dance with the world. You are more than equal to any challenge. Embrace the challenges of life, and march forth in the faith that you can achieve all things.

Charmaine Smith, Esq. is a practicing lawyer with a specialty in early intervention for children. She spends much of her spare time mentoring youth offenders aged eleven to nineteen, helping to positively reintegrate them into the community. She is also an expert in housing law and has advocated extensively on behalf of low-income clients with rent arrears and other debt issues. Charmaine is a noted public speaker, and has found tremendous success voicing the concerns of her varied clients to the public. Connect with Charmaine at www.CharmaineSmith.com.

Ricky Young

I AM THE GREATEST

Growing up, I admired Muhammad Ali. He was my first inspiration to box. Ali was the greatest in the ring, and for a couple of reasons. First, he worked very, very hard. He loved training, he loved running, he loved working out. And he had that *belief.* He was famous for saying, "I am the greatest." He convinced himself that he was the greatest—and he became the greatest.

To step in the ring like Ali, you have to take yourself to another place, someplace you may never have been before. I've had people tell me that my face looks different when I'm in the ring. It's almost like you have to hypnotize yourself, to psych yourself up and reach down deep within yourself to find that champion inside you, and pull that champion out. You are the greatest. Somebody could try to be you, but nobody could be a greater *you* than you. You are the greatest *you,* so you are the greatest.

As a kid, I was also inspired by the 1976 United States Olympic team. It might be the greatest boxing team ever. It had one silver medalist, one bronze medalist, and five gold medalists. Those five are some of the greatest names in the history of the sport: Sugar Ray Leonard, Michael Spinks, Leon Spinks, Howard Davis, Jr. and Leo Randolph. My other inspiration was my neighborhood—Harlem. I knew how important it was to know how to defend myself. And I could, to a degree, but the time came when I said, *You know, I want there to be no doubt when I have a situation.* Learning how to box was my "no doubt."

Achievement starts in your mind. What do you want? How can you go after your dream if you don't know what the dream is? First and foremost, you need to know what you want. And if you don't, you need to make discovering it a full-time job. What do you want? What do you enjoy doing so much that when you're doing it, time seems to stop; when you look up and hours have gone by? What's happening when you're in the zone? Your dream is something you're so passionate about, you would do it for free.

I signed up for the Golden Gloves, an amateur boxing tournament in New York. I had no idea what I was doing. I sent in an application, and they sent back the date I needed to show up for my fight. They also sent me a list of gyms where I should go to train. I didn't even know I *needed* to train. So I didn't even show up for my fight. But I did go to a gym—PAL (Police Athletic League) Gym on 52nd Street.

At the PAL Gym, I found out I had some talent. So I signed up again for the Golden Gloves. My coach was Bob McQuiller, and he was special. As a boxer, he beat three world champions. He had worked in Ali's camp and even trained Miles Davis. People called Bobby "Mr. Poetry in Motion" because he was so quick and graceful in the ring. I was amazed watching him show me moves. At sixty-three he still moved with that same speed and grace. He taught me the science of the sport. He also taught me the importance of preparation and confidence.

The night of my first amateur match, I went to the arena, and I was calm, but I knew at some point I'd get nervous. It was in Madison Square Garden, and a lot of people from my neighborhood came to watch. I told myself, *When I see Bobby get nervous, I'll get nervous.* So I watched Bobby. I waited for him to get nervous, but he never did. We got in the ring; we got closer and closer to the bell, but Bob stayed relaxed. I looked at him and I could just tell that he knew everything he taught me would work, and if I just did that, I'd be successful. When I won, I felt like Ali—I felt like I was the greatest.

I got into boxing seriously when I started training at Gleason's gym. I trained with passion: running, doing a ton of ring work, bag work, push-ups, sit-ups. I was so disciplined I even changed my diet, eating nothing but fresh food. And it all felt tremendous, especially when I got into the ring. There's so much joy in training for something, working for something and then achieving it. When I got into the ring, it was always about winning. I had to

> *You are the greatest you, so you are the greatest.*

win that fight no matter what. And whenever I had the attitude, *I have to win this match,* I won, but I won because of my preparation and training. Like Ali, I worked really hard. When you prepare, you're preparing to win. Not just compete, but win. Winning isn't the beginning of the journey, though it may be the beginning of something bigger. All that preparation before the win, that's the journey.

I always felt great, waiting for that bell to ring, because I got into the zone. I psyched myself up; I convinced myself I could do it. And then this calm came over me, and I took action and got the endorphins moving. When I stepped into the ring, I had to go into a hypnotic state. I had to visualize success, visualize winning. I had to reach down deep inside myself to bring out the champion in me. There was no room for doubt, no room for negative thoughts.

So I would keep moving, dancing around the ring as if I was in a trance, shaking out the nervousness. I even went into the other guy's corner. I'd shadow box in his area, and the other guy would be as nervous as you-know-what. Here I'd be, not nervous. A calm would come over me. You use psychology on yourself, and you use it on your opponent. I learned that from watching Ali—he was at his best when he was dancing around the ring. You couldn't touch him. To him, boxing was an art and a science. And I learned that from Bobby.

But moving isn't important only inside the ring. To achieve your dreams, you've got to move, even if all you do is make a phone call that will help you get closer to your dream. You have to psych yourself out to get in that ring, because it's a scary thing! If you don't put yourself in the zone, you're going to be in trouble. When you get in there, you could be knocked out. You could be hurt. You could be killed. So you really have to be prepared. You've got

> *If you're going to get from where you are to where you want to be, you've got to move!*

a lot on the line. Train for your dreams. Practice, practice, practice so that when you get into your ring, your moves will be second nature. If you're going to get from where you are to where you want to be, you've got to move!

I told Bobby I wanted to compete in the Empire State Games, which is a mini-Olympics for New York. He said I wasn't ready because all of the other fighters had a lot of experience. Some had dozens of fights behind them; I had competed in just two fights. In Golden Gloves, if you've fought less than five matches, then you fight someone who's had less than five matches. But at the Empire State Games, I might have to fight someone with seventy matches. But I begged Bobby, and he said, "Okay."

I competed in four New York regional matches, and I won them all: two knockouts, two decisions. My opponents had more experience than I did, but I beat them anyway. So I was sent to Syracuse for my final two matches, and I won those, too. I was the Empire State Games champion! Before the games, I didn't know I was going to win, but I was confident. Going to the gym day after day and training hard gave me the confidence I needed to fight and to win. And it put me in the zone where everything just worked; everything was going in slow motion and in everything I tried, every punch I threw, I was in the flow. The key to achieving your dream is self-discipline. When you can master this, you're really working with something. Self-discipline is persistence in action.

The Olympic training coach was from Syracuse, and he saw me fight. He invited me to the Olympic training center in Colorado Springs, Colorado, and I trained there before I turned pro. And then I became a professional boxer, and realized my first big dream. I won eighteen out of twenty-two matches.

No matter what your dream is, it's achievable. Some people stop short of achieving their dreams because they have fear, or it's hard for them to accept they're the greatest at anything, whatever their dream is. Jim Rohn said, "You may not be able to do all you find out, but make sure you find out all you can do."

We need to empower and affirm our children. We need to tell them, "You are a champion. You are great. You are super-intelligent. You can do anything you want to do, anything you want to achieve." We need to teach children responsibility, and how to train for their dream. If we don't, then later they won't be ready to get in the ring, or willing to fight for their dreams. You have to

> *You have to believe in yourself, believe you can do it. If you don't believe, you won't even start to fight. And if there's anything worth fighting for, it's your dreams.*

believe in yourself, believe you can do it. If you don't believe, you won't even start to fight. And if there's anything worth fighting for, it's your dreams.

Yes, the stakes are high. In fact, it *is* a matter of life or death, fighting or not fighting for your dreams. Step into the ring of life. So many people will be affected either way. If you go for your dreams, so many people are going to be uplifted, inspired and encouraged to go after their own dreams and be their greatest selves. They might even see you, as I saw Muhammad Ali on TV, and say, "Wow. I want to do something great."

Jack Dempsey said, "If you get knocked down, you get up even when you can't." And my friend Willy Jolley, The Comeback King, said, "A setback is a setup for a comeback." You've got to have that passion, that determination that nothing is going to stop you. And you've got to be bold and take action. Don't worry about failing. If you fail, so what? Try it again and again. Train your mind to step into the ring and say, *I'm not going to stop. I want this, and I'm going to go for it.*

When I taught boxing conditioning at Columbia University in New York City, I would ask my students, "Are you the greatest?" They almost always said "no," to which I would reply, "No one walking on this planet can be a greater you than YOU. Not one person. You are the greatest YOU." Then, I would repeat the question. "Are you the greatest?" Almost everyone said "yes."

When you ask yourself, *Am I worthy? What if I'm not good enough? What if I fail?* remember, no one can be a greater you than you. *You* are the greatest!

Ricky Young grew up in Harlem, competed in the Golden Gloves and was an Empire State Games champion before training at the US Olympic Training Center in Colorado Springs and becoming a professional boxer. He taught boxing at Columbia University for eleven years, and continues to teach boxing today. Ricky is also an accomplished inspirational speaker and hosts the motivational radio talk show, "What's in Your Hand" (www.whcr.org/SHOW_PROFILE/whats_in_ your_hand). Broadcasting from City College in New York, Ricky interviews authors, entrepreneurs and high achievers and shares the universal success principles he learned in the ring.

Vickie Roundtree

FIGHTING MY WAY OUT OF FEAR

One day, when I was a freshman in high school, a bully followed me home from school with a whole slew of her relatives. They shouted and called me names. "I'm going to kick your butt!" the girl yelled. I walked faster with fear seeping into every cell of my body. "Every time I see you, I'm going to kick your ___!"

It was day two of this nonsense, and I realized: *This is not going to go away.* She had come to school looking for me the day before, but since I got out early, she didn't find me. I looked around for my friends, cousins, anybody—of course they were nowhere to be found. I took a deep breath and thought, *Okay. Either I live the rest of my life in fear of this girl, or I face my fear and fight like there's no tomorrow.* I threw my books down on the ground and put up my dukes. And then I had to deal with another layer of fear. I thought, *She's much bigger than I am. It'll all be over if she hits me first—I need to take the first swing.* I did. We tussled.

Many say I won the fight; I'm not really sure. All I know is, once I took action, my fear went away instantly. And when the fight was over, I knew I would never be afraid of her again. Facing my fear and feeling it disappear was a valuable life lesson. Unfortunately, the lesson didn't really sink in until many years later, when I finally fought the big bully in my mind that kept me from loving myself, knowing myself and knowing my own self-worth—my own mother.

My mother was extremely controlling and manipulative, and I lived in fear of her empty threats. Growing up, I wasn't taught to be self-sufficient, to pursue my dreams or even have dreams of my own; I was her, and she raised me as an extension of herself. She needed constant attention, and my world was built around making sure she got it. She convinced me that nothing I did was right—to feel *I'm not good enough.* It seemed that every happy moment and milestone in my life was one of sadness to her.

When I was eighteen, I wanted to go off to college more than anything. But my mother didn't want me to go. Every time I tried to become independent or pursue my own dream, she either dangled a carrot in front of my face or put the fear of God into me. "You're going to need me someday," she would say. "You're going to need *me* before I ever need *you.*" Those words penetrated so deeply, they stopped me dead in my tracks. I had become accustomed to being fearful.

Mine was no ordinary young adulthood. I felt like Rapunzel, trapped in her tower. Every year or so, I would try to break away from my mother, but I didn't succeed until after our huge fight when I was twenty-seven years old and still living at home. When I left, slamming the door, she shouted, "Fine! Leave! And never come back!" I knew it was true: *I will never live in that house with her again.*

But even then I was bound by fear. Even though I had physically left home, in my heart and my mind I was still trapped in the tower. The internal impact my mother had on me was about control, and unconsciously, feeling frightened and trapped dictated many of my actions going forward. *What if she was right, and someday I come crawling back to her after all?* If I had to, I didn't want to have to crawl too far. I only moved two miles away.

For many years, I had some real self-esteem issues. I didn't know who I was—I wasn't used to understanding or expressing my own feelings, or believing I was a whole person. Therefore, I spent the next several years after I left my mother's house in and out of toxic relationships. I didn't know that I was someone, that I had gifts to bring to the world. I was still looking for that love I needed, that attention, from people who did not have my best interests at heart.

Early on, I wanted to become a journalist and be on the news. I remember someone telling me, "If you do that, you'll have to move to some hick town far away from your family, where you'll be the only African-American." I was used to living in fear and choosing not to act because of it; so my immediate response was one of fear: *Oh, God! Well then, I'm not doing that!* I let someone else stop my

> *Many say I won the fight; I'm not really sure. All I know is, once I took action, my fear went away instantly. And when the fight was over, I knew I would never be afraid of her again.*

dream cold—and I let that be my pattern going forward. Because I didn't know or value myself enough to pursue my heart's desires, I ended up going to school for business. I listened to the voices that told me what was expected, what *they* thought was practical.

For twenty-six years, I worked in the business world. But I always felt unhappy. I'd be sitting at a baseball game, thinking, *What's wrong with me? Everybody ought to be happy at a baseball game! Why am I not having any fun?* I had done everything society had told me to do—gone to business school, made a successful career, bought a house. At gatherings, people often told me, "Wow, I'd love to have your job." I had all the bells and whistles, but I still felt there was something terribly wrong with my life.

In 2009, after I spent ten lucrative years with the same company, a separation package was offered for those of us who wanted to volunteer to take it. This was at the height of the recession, when the news was reporting almost daily that this or that company had laid off four thousand workers, two thousand. Ford plants were closing, banks were failing, the world seemed to be in total chaos— and I still raised my hand.

People thought I was insane, but for once, I simply had to listen to myself. *Fear is just a feeling,* my internal voice told me again, for the first time since I'd fought that bully. *It's now or never.*

There's a saying: "You can't see the picture when you're in the frame." And when I stepped outside of it, when I left the tower and took a chance on myself as an entrepreneur, a coach and a speaker, I found my gift—I'm finally doing what I was born to do. In the corporate world, I was just helping the stockholders and the corporation. No wonder I hated my life! I was living a script that wasn't written for me. Helping to add value to other people's lives, I'm elated. I have the capacity, now, to share basic life and leadership skills with others so they can live better lives earlier—skills I was never taught but had to develop after years of living trapped in low self-esteem and in others' perceptions.

> *When I finally decided I'd had enough, I released the people that didn't contribute to my growth as a person, including my mother. I said a prayer and let them all fly away, realizing it was necessary for my survival.*

Life now is more beautiful than I ever imagined it could be. I feel free for the first time ever. If you can imagine being trapped in a tower for twenty-six years and then being set free, that's what it feels like to be living my dream. I've let go of that internal, bullying voice; I've let go of all the door-blockers, and on the other side of the door, I found my dream educating and inspiring others to live their dreams.

When I finally decided I'd had enough, I released the people that didn't contribute to my growth as a person, including my mother. I said a prayer and let them all fly away, realizing it was necessary for my survival. For years I couldn't understand why I felt so trapped and miserable, and why I went through all the craziness with toxic people. I asked, *Why, why, why?* Now I get it. I had to learn how to fight my way out of fear in order to get strong and express my gifts. God knew that I would be a speaker, and a voice for others to learn and grow from. I thank God for my journey. Now that I understand my path, there is no bitterness left in my heart—just sheer gratitude for all of my life experiences. Without them, I would not be the person I am now.

Know yourself: you have undeniable value. Know what you want and what is true to your heart. If there are people in your life who are not supportive of you, it is time to evaluate whether or not

> *Look back on your life and think about all those times you pressed past your fears. You won! You're still here!*

they belong in your life. It doesn't matter what the relationship is; it's about the boundaries. And if people cross the boundaries you have set, it should be a warning: *I need to do something about this.* Be aware.

Fear is just a feeling: once you've fought your way past the fear, it's gone. Don't let fear be a factor. When you choose to act instead, it puts you in a place of power and gives you the self-confidence to live your dreams. The more you face fear, the less fear you will feel. You don't even need to let it into your world. Look back on your life and think about all those times you pressed past your fears. You won! You're still here!

Fear is not tangible, it's not physical. It's just a feeling. But people treat it as if it's a place they're locked inside forever. And if they don't know they possess the key to their own release, they won't try to find their way out.

You can stay away from dream-stealers. You can fight your way out of any circumstances that do not align with your dreams and hopes. Push past fear. Joy, peace and hope for tomorrow are on the other side. So listen to that voice that's saying you should be doing more—don't leave this earth with your dreams untold.

Vickie Roundtree grew up in Illinois, graduated from Lewis University with a BS in business administration and worked in corporate America for twenty-six years, holding increasingly responsible positions from sales and marketing to information technology. Fulfilling her entrepreneur spirit, she and her husband Torrence established Fortrees International, a debt-buying company that is generating a significant stream of passive income for themselves and their investors, allowing both of them the freedom to do what they love. Now, Vickie is living her dream as a successful entrepreneur and inspirational speaker, teamed with John Maxwell's Coaching & Speaking certification program. Vickie is currently writing her first book, Take A Chance on Yourself. *Vickie's favorite African proverb, "lift as you climb," guides her in service to Operation Smile (www.OperationSmile.org), an organization that performs necessary surgeries for children born with cleft lips or cleft palates. Connect with Vickie at www.TheCoachYouNeed.com.*

Alexis Williams-Patton

A God-Given Dream

I sat in church one Sunday, my head bowed, praying hard for the Lord's guidance in the face of great hurt, anger and disappointment. My husband and I had just broken up, and I was left to raise our two young boys. My heart was broken. Marriage is a sacred covenant. All married people have disagreements and misunderstandings—why did that mean we had to get a divorce?

The breakup of my marriage was devastating, and the fact that it came six months after the loss of my beloved mother made my grief overwhelming. Over a time of much prayer, I realized I was fighting a battle—a spiritual fight, for my future. This fight was for my destiny and my purpose on Earth. As I prayed that Sunday and searched my soul, asking the Lord, "Why did this *truly* happen to me?" a guest speaker was introduced and began his sermon. I felt my soul reverberate with his words: "Each of us has an assignment here on earth—a God-given assignment."

I had never heard that before, and it resonated deep within my spirit. I came home and spent some time with the Lord, prayed, read my Bible and got all of the guest minister's teaching materials. I studied, and began to have a revelation about his message. Jeremiah 29:11 says, "I have known you; even before you were formed in your mother's womb, I had a plan for you. I have called you to be a voice for the nations, a mouthpiece of hope and encouragement to the world." I heard the Lord say, "Give back to others. Esteem others more highly than yourself by helping them to realize their dreams." I thought, "Wow! God has always had an intent, for everybody's life—it's just that some people have found their original intent and plan and purpose, and some have strayed and gone in a different direction."

I had the best parents a child could ever have. The love and encouragement I received from them was matchless, and I try always to model it with my own children—and others. My most beautiful memory is of my mother's smiling face. Arneatha Williams—my mother—had a smile on her face every day of her life, a deep and shining smile for everyone she met. Really. She never had a down day. And when I was grieving her death and the loss of my marriage, when it seemed as if my heart would tear in two, I asked the Lord, "Why was she always smiling?" "Because," He said, "her dreams were realized."

Back in the 1950s and 60s, it was common practice for doctors to perform hysterectomies on black women, and purposely sterilize them without their consent. My mother was one of these women. When it was discovered that the twins she was carrying had died, the doctor performed a hysterectomy on her instead of a D & C. And when she heard what he had done, she was devastated. She would never again have the chance to bear a child. From that moment forward, she just could not imagine her life without a child—the only thing she'd ever wanted, her greatest dream, was to have a baby.

One day in the mid-1960s, my father came home and told her he knew of a place where they could adopt a baby. That baby was me. She always told me, "You are the best thing that has ever happened to me. Because I have you, I am complete. And I am so happy." From the moment my parents brought me home, my mother had no reason to be sad. She was always happy.

After she passed, I thought of my mother all the time and conjured up her smile to help me through each day. *How would she handle this situation?* She always told me, "You don't say you hate people. Say you don't like their ways, but don't say you *hate* them." My parents said, "Treat everybody right, even when they don't treat you right. God will deal with them." "Do the right thing. Right always wins." They always tried to teach me what Jesus had taught: forgiveness and compassion.

Since I was a little girl, I've known that I wanted to help people. I am named after my father, Alex, and my name, Alexis, means "helper of mankind." My mother told me how I always used to bring home all of the abandoned dogs, cats and children in my

> *From the moment my parents brought me home, my mother had no reason to be sad. She was always happy.*

neighborhood, wanting to take care of them. After seeing me in a sixth grade speech contest, my father told me many times that my voice would bring me before an audience. I believe my parents sensed and knew my assignment long before I did.

Oftentimes, your parents or others can see your purpose and assignment in you when you're a child. However, negative spiritual forces come into everyone's life to divert them from God's original intention. God has *always* had good plans for mankind. And God gives most of us dreams and visions of who we are supposed to be when we're little children. It's just that, sometimes, it takes more than one person, event or resource to help guide you to your original intended path and higher calling.

For the past twenty-three years I have walked close to God, totally committed to following scripture and trying to pattern my life according to the Bible. I learned early on that it is scriptural to be a giver; it was scriptural to discover my destiny and purpose. There are those in the Bible who started out on the wrong path, but through both hardship and triumph, God ultimately orchestrated their lives.

People like Jonah, Esther, David, Joseph, Ruth and the Queen of Sheba didn't set out on the original paths God had intended for them, but ultimately, each of them ended up just where He wanted. Esther was trying to discover her destiny and ended up marrying the king. The Queen of Sheba went to King Solomon for counsel, and although he was the wealthiest man in the world, she was wise enough to take him an offering; when she left him, "she left with more than she ever had." The Bible is full of serious stories of destiny and purpose, stories about people who were on a journey and discovered who they were as they obeyed God. But I

> *Dreams are spiritual—they come from God. Therefore, fighting for your dreams is spiritual, not physical.*

did not understand until about ten years ago, when I asked to see my path and heard the Lord's words, that I was still being called. I was being called to be a blessing of encouragement and hope to others.

The idea to host an encouragement conference, "Women of Destiny, Purpose and Truth," came to me in 2002. I felt compelled to share with other women that there *is* hope and an exciting new life ahead, no matter what hardships they have been through. The conference was a life-changing experience. And though it was for others to feel blessed and encouraged, it was also for me, to step out of the self-pity and despair I felt after my two terrible losses. Since then, I've held the conference every two years and begun writing several books. My father's vision, of my voice bringing me before an audience, is coming true.

You too came here with a dream in your heart, and you have a purpose, no matter the disappointment, difficulty or pain you have gone through—many of us have. And that's the Good News. You are not alone.

The conception of your dream has already happened, just like in the parable from the Bible: Elizabeth had conceived a baby, but it wasn't until Mary came along and said, "You're pregnant!" that the baby began to leap within her. She needed somebody to confirm her reality. So seek out the voices of hope, the modern-day Marys of the Earth who can tell you, "I know that baby is in you. And it can leap now. You will know God's promise for your life." Feel that baby leap! Nurture it, talk to it. Tell it, "You shall come to pass."

Dreams are spiritual—they come from God. Therefore, fighting for your dreams is spiritual, not physical. There's a Bible scripture that says, "We struggle not against flesh and blood, but against principalities and powers of darkness." We all have to take action, but we get tripped up when we forget that the real journey is within, and beyond physical occurrences. We must meet our spiritual challenges with actions based in spirit—only then can we fulfill our dreams.

We're not fighting against each other, or against our circumstances. The fight is against those forces that do not want us to fulfill our purpose on Earth: to be a blessing to others, to bring words of encouragement and hope. We all have that spiritual fight against old voices of rejection, disappointment, hurt and pain, but

> *Every morning now I wake up joyful and excited, knowing that I am a gift to the world.*

we must refuse to play the game with those feelings. It's time to say no to the voices that say, "You can't," and to fight against the dream-killers of low self-esteem and fear. They are just feelings that, if not checked at the gate, will stop you from getting on your original flight to the wonderful destiny God has for you.

When I feel that fear rise within me, I always think, *Okay, what am I here for?* And I remember God's original intent for my life: to be a voice of encouragement and hope.

I too needed somebody to be there for me when I was down and scrambling, searching for answers. I always found that rock in my parents, especially my mother; and though she has passed, she is still with me, encouraging me and watching over me. I know she would tell me that even if I reach only one person, my voice is enough to bring hope.

Every morning now I wake up joyful and excited, knowing that I am a gift to the world. It has been almost thirteen years since my mother's death and the divorce, and still, whenever my two sons and our relatives and I get together, we always talk about my mother's big, beautiful smile, and how she had truly found her path in life. Her joy helped heal everyone she encountered.

Of course there will be challenges to face, and sorrows to endure—but as my mother would say, you have to fight to be happy when you have down days. You lost your job? Be happy—another one is just around the corner. You lost a loved one? You can still be happy, for you loved each other well. Surround yourself with the dream-makers, the joyous ones, and listen well to the voice of your God-given spirit. Fight for your destiny and you too will realize your dreams.

God has an assignment just for you. You already have that big dream within you—you have ever since you arrived here on Earth. It is only waiting for you to step up and fight for it.

Alexis Patton is a sought-after inspirational speaker, an author and the founder of Women of Destiny, Purpose and Truth Conferences®. She has worked as a senior recruiter for Fortune 500 companies, and since 1995 has owned and operated several small businesses that have employed over twenty-five women who were previously unemployed or on welfare. Her book, Keep Moving Forward and Upward: Pressing Towards Your Higher Calling is forthcoming in December 2011. Alexis is currently developing several non-profit organizations for single parents, and a literacy group for aspiring urban adult and youth writers. She is also completing her Master's in human resource management. She lives in Northern California with her two teenage sons, Isaiah and Xavier. Connect with Alexis at www. AlexisWilliamsPattonEnterprises.com.

Joseph J. Rangel

BECOMING A
STUDENT OF LIFE

When I was a young boy of nine or ten, one of my chores was walking the family dog, Bob the Boxer. I loved this ritual; the quiet time exploring the neighborhood allowed me to contemplate possibilities, letting my imagination soar and wonder what the future would bring.

We lived in a typical, modest two-story house in Los Angeles, California, perched between "good" and "bad" neighborhoods. On one side was a neighborhood of graffiti and gangs, scary in its disorder and decay. On the other, one block away, was the upscale Wilshire district, site of mansions, neatly kept lawns and movie stars.

On many of my walks with Bob we'd find ourselves across Pico Boulevard in the nice part of town, admiring the large, beautifully kept houses and marveling at the people who lived in them. One in particular caught my eye; every weekend the glamorous occupants seemed to be having a party. Lamborghinis, Ferraris and other exotic cars spilled out their cargos of movie stars and sports figures. Right then and there I resolved to make something of myself, to find a way to achieve that lifestyle. I thought, *I want this. I want to be successful, and live a life full of possibilities.*

My parents had always told me to work hard, get through school and go on to get a college education, so that's what I did. I worked hard enough to finish college early, at nineteen years old. I was young, ready and hungry, and certain of the success I felt I deserved. Unfortunately, the world didn't feel quite the same way, and I met rejection after rejection. I just couldn't find a job, no matter how hard I tried. One potential employer would tell me I was overqualified, the next that I was under-qualified. I felt lied to and cheated, frustrated at the lack of payoff from my hard work and early accomplishment.

My father always said, "You are the same as the people you associate with." Looking around me I realized I needed to surround myself with different, more motivated people. Whenever I talked of my dreams my friends would say, "You're crazy," and mock my desire to make something of myself. I started cultivating friendships with successful people who inspired me to be better than what I was.

At the age of twenty I decided to get my real estate license. *This is it. I'm on my way,* I thought. But while my license got me into a firm, I still was a young-looking, inexperienced kid. Clients would let me show them houses, but then ask to be switched to an older, more experienced agent to close the deal. Not only was this humiliating, but I couldn't make a living. *This is so frustrating! There's nothing I can do to change this, except get older.*

I decided to turn my frustration into a motivator, to use frustration to take me where I wanted to go. I started focusing on solutions rather than problems. I observed and learned from all the successful people I surrounded myself with. I quickly realized, *If I'm going to be as smart as the more experienced agents, it's going to take time, preparation and study to become more knowledgeable about the industry and the marketplace.* I started focusing less on "the pitch" and more on listening to my clients' needs. What type of house did they dream of, what lifestyle were they aspiring to, what wishes did they have that I could fulfill?

Since I'd never been very good at sales (my lack of success in job hunting was a prime example), I figured I had to do something different. I applied myself diligently to develop a victorious attitude, and I started to see myself victorious. I began wearing suits every day to separate myself from the other agents. I started coaching people on how they could live that lifestyle they deserved to have. All by listening instead of talking and absorbing lessons from the oddest places even while teaching others.

When I encounter failure I understand that failure is temporary, and it can act like a teacher. You learn what you are doing wrong, correct it and keep trying with a different approach. Even though I began to see success as a realtor at a typical company, around this time I realized that if I was going to fulfill my dream I had to

> *When I encounter failure I understand that failure is temporary, and it can act like a teacher. You learn what you are doing wrong, correct it and keep trying with a different approach.*

change my approach. I began to see a pattern. My age kept getting in the way of fulfilling my dreams. *I have to change the rules and succeed in my own way,* I thought.

My father always worked for himself; he always led by action. He demonstrated the value of hard work and the rewards one receives when you don't quit, no matter how bad things get. He always told me, "Son, never give up. Never give up," and, "Have passion for what you do." He inspired me to work for myself. I've never been afraid of hard work or risk. So I became an innovator and I learned the real estate investment business and I moved forward.

At twenty-one, I started my own company, a firm handling real estate investments. I became passionate about real estate. I was excited and nervous at the same time, because I had no idea what the outcome would be. But I understood the law of averages. *If other real estate investors are successful, there's no reason I can't be successful just like them,* I reasoned. I knew if I was confident, disciplined and worked hard enough, I would succeed. I just had to build momentum and then stay focused so I wouldn't lose the momentum.

I may have been young, and looked even younger, but as the head of my own business, I thought that didn't matter. It is said that tough times don't last, but tough people do. I used my talents, will and persistence to see those obstacles as just another set of problems to confront. And confront them I did, watching my little company grow and prosper despite the obstacles presented by external factors.

For years now, I've kept a "vision board" in my home and office. I use this to remind myself of my goals, dreams and desires. I see it in the morning when I wake up, at night when I go to bed and at many times during the day. It really helps me sort out the who, how and what in my life, which lets me keep track of where I'm going and how I'm going to get there.

Later in life I was grateful that I didn't have an opportunity, because if someone had given me a job back then my life would have been different. Because no one wanted to help me, I kept fighting and eventually founded my own company, which allowed

> *Later in life I was grateful that I didn't have an opportunity, because if someone had given me a job back then my life would have been different. Because no one wanted to help me, I kept fighting and eventually founded my own company, which allowed me to achieve my dreams.*

me to achieve my dreams. I bought my first house in an upscale, gated community at age twenty-four, and within a year had flipped it for a bigger one. Shortly after that, as I strolled through my new neighborhood with my new dog, Louie the Poodle, I couldn't help staring at all the lovely houses and well-kept lawns. The old soundtrack began to play in my head: *If only I could have this too.* Then it hit me—*these people are my neighbors. I'm actually one of them.*

As I passed one especially nice house on my block, the homeowner caught site of me and came out front to talk. "Hey, beautiful dog," he enthusiastically blurted, "we keep poodles too, who's your breeder?" It took me a moment to realize the homeowner wasn't looking at me like a stranger, like I didn't belong. He was just coming out to talk to his neighbor—me. I had done it! I'd achieved my dream, first crystallized on that long-ago walk with Bob the Boxer.

With each new dream came another obstacle, blocking me from achieving my new goals. Each new obstacle required innovative thinking to overcome its novel challenges. Yet the old standbys— hard work, humility and willingness to try new things—all combined to allow me to overcome each different obstacle in my

> *Success is not the materialistic possessions you obtain in life, but rather the person you become in pursuit of that success.*

path. I once heard this great expression that has proven true for me: "The harder you work the luckier you get. Develop a winner's attitude. The winner never quits and the quitter never wins."

To me, failure has been a blessing in disguise. Failure can teach you things; it can help you to succeed in spite of your naysayers. You have to make your own opportunities at every turn. I refused to allow failure to hold me back, and learned to use it as a teacher. Falling just made me more determined to get up and try again, a different and better way. I work seven days a week, but to me it doesn't seem like work because I love what I do. You must love what you are doing if you want to become successful. You will never be successful, or happy and healthy, if you don't love what you do. Success is not the materialistic possessions you obtain in life, but rather the person you become in pursuit of that success.

When a roadblock appears, hit it hard. Each time you bounce off, try again, but with a different approach, until finally, you're able to blast through and reach the road ahead. Then cruise that road toward your dreams until you hit yet another roadblock. Setbacks can be the catalysts that transform failure into success. Cherish them, for they are life's greatest teachers. Roadblocks force you to try something different. Use them as an opportunity to change your method, and keep trying until you succeed.

Those who learn from failure achieve the greatest successes. Change your approach as you try again, until you hit on the path that works. Hard work is essential, but not enough. Be humble enough to realize that you can learn from everyone you encounter. Be open to new ideas and learn something new every day. Become a student of life. And keep following your dreams, even as they change. Anything you think of doing is possible, no matter what anyone else tells you.

Take that first step, do whatever it takes and you will succeed. You only become a failure when you quit trying. Never give up and never stop trying. Dreams come true only if you *really* want them, and if you fight for them. Always fight for your dreams and never give up.

Joseph J. Rangel is among the top real-estate investors in Southern California. After completing high school and college early, he started his own company at the age of twenty-one and in four short years reached his childhood goal of becoming a millionaire. Through his public speaking engagements and workshops, Joseph empowers aspiring entrepreneurs and real estate agents. He is currently writing a book for people who want to learn how to make money investing in real estate. Connect with Joseph at www. JosephRangel.com.

HONOR THE GREATNESS WITHIN

M arc and I were best friends since the third grade. We had a big group of friends, but he was my closest friend growing up. We used to hang out in his backyard, talking and laughing for hours and hours as we played one-on-one basketball with his little six-foot hoop. He was the funniest person I knew, and he had a way of bringing people together. He was so magnetic. Everybody loved Marc.

As we got older and got busy with life, work and moving around, we sometimes lost touch for a month or two. But we would always reconnect so easily, as if no time had passed, and everything would seem as it always had. At one point about seven years ago, I thought, *I need to call Marc.* It had been a little while since we'd spoken. He had gone through a few different jobs in recent years, trying to find his niche. When we had last talked he said he wasn't that happy with his current job. So I felt inspired to tell him about what I'd been doing with my ministry and helping other people. I thought he might be inspired, too. But instead of calling him when I thought about it, I waited.

Maybe a little over a week later, a mutual friend of ours called. "I think I heard some news about Marc," he said. "But I don't know if it's *our* Marc. I think you should call his mom and see what's going on." So I did. And she told me, through her tears, that Marc had committed suicide. He was in his early thirties. I was shocked, to say the least. I was devastated. My best friend was gone. Why hadn't I called?

Immediately, I wondered what would have happened if I had called him. One phone conversation may not be able to save someone's life, but what if that one call *had* made a difference? I knew Marc wasn't having the easiest time, but I'd had no idea what he was really going through. If he had known how much he was loved, regarded and valued, how important he was in the world, would he have killed himself?

One of the hardest things I ever did in my life was the eulogy at Marc's funeral. In the pulpit of a church in San Francisco, I looked out over the great mass of faces gathered to mourn Marc's passing and struggled to keep my emotions under control so I could guide the service as a celebration of his life. I was the minister, so that was my job—but it was one thing to do it for someone I didn't

> *I was shocked, to say the least. I was devastated. My best friend was gone. Why hadn't I called?*

know and another to do it for someone I had been so close to. I'd stayed up for forty-eight hours composing the eulogy, searching for the right words. Searching for what I could say that would be a comfort and a blessing to Marc's friends and family as well as to Marc himself—even though he couldn't physically hear me. I wanted both to honor my best friend and to share with everyone that there is great hope in life.

"Marc was a good guy," I said to the congregation and the crowd. "There weren't many people he didn't get along with. If you really needed something and he had it or could get it, he would help you out. He was never a phony, and he didn't allow us to be phony around him either. He had a presumably tough exterior, but he had a truly soft interior. And he had grit—even though he could be playfully stubborn in an argument, he'd always make you think at least two or three times about your own views.

"And he was a glue guy," I continued. "He brought people together. You knew Marc; you knew his personality. He was such a fun-loving guy, so lovable and open. Looking around us today, we see people of every age, ethnicity and background. Maybe, in a normal situation, we would not all gather together. But this one man is our common link, because of who he was. Maybe, had we been able to tap into that gift and let him know just how great he was, the sky would have been the limit.

"We need to share with each other how we really feel about each other more often," I said, "and what a difference we make, how important we are in the world. If Marc had known what an impact he made on all our lives, that might have been the spark he needed to boost his self-worth."

When Marc died, I was so stunned that if you asked me, "Gary, how are you? Where are you standing?" I wouldn't have been able tell you. And I started to blame myself. But I realized pretty quickly that if I didn't take an inventory of myself, it would be just that simple for me to begin an *emotional* suicide.

Physical suicide is only one kind of suicide—people commit spiritual, financial and even emotional suicide all the time, unable to make good on the promise of their own defined destiny-direction out of a lack of self-worth, like Marc. You blame yourself, you feel guilty, you start a downward spiral of negativity. So I had to do a kind of checklist with my own life, my own destiny. *What didn't I do?* I didn't call him when I felt I should have. I had to own up to that. *What could I have done? Could I have reached into him more?* Yes, I could have.

To me, there's a certain sense of follow-through in your destiny and calling. I was doing it up to a point, through the ministry, the church and helping people—but I could've reached out to more of my friends and said, "Hey, take a look at what we've been through. We were blessed to make it through our teenage years—let's look at what's going to happen going forward." I didn't do that. I didn't do it in an internal way, nor did I do it in a way that it could be seen on a large scale.

And that, right there, is what drives me now. I can't get that time back. So what do I have within me to make things better going forward? I can strive to be a blessing to as many people in this world as possible, to let them know how great they are, one way or another.

I realized for years that I had the potential to do great things, but I would switch the light bulb off unconsciously. Or unplug myself and never commit, never really complete. That is, until about a year ago, during the worst snowstorm the D.C. area had seen in

> *Physical suicide is only one kind of suicide—people commit spiritual, financial and even emotional suicide all the time, unable to make good on the promise of their own defined destiny-direction out of a lack of self-worth, like Marc.*

decades. Being from California, I'd never seen anything like it. Stuck in my apartment by myself, I was unable to go anywhere or do anything. There was nothing on TV—it was just me, God and three feet of snow. Sitting there, looking out the window, I started talking to God about my life, and realizing: *I have to step up to the plate, or I'm dishonoring myself, I'm dishonoring God, I'm dishonoring the greatness within me, I'm dishonoring what I committed to when Marc passed away. Nobody,* it hit me, *has to die for me to reach my destiny.*

As I watched people outside dig their cars out, making paths so they could get out of the parking lot and on the road to wherever they were going, I clearly saw my destiny: to help people figure out and work through the process of digging themselves out of sub-par lives. I can't do it for them, but I can hand them a shovel, maybe a scraper to clear their heart's windshield. Fulfilling their destiny—that was up to them.

I thought I had cabin fever, but it turns out it was constructive faith. That moment ignited something within me, and I haven't looked back.

Your windshield is larger than your rearview mirror—what's ahead of you is much greater than what's behind you. The first thing to do is to take inventory, and be honest with yourself about where you are. You can set a destination in your GPS, but if you don't have a starting location, it can't map out your journey. You won't know where you're going unless you understand where you are. Once you understand that, then you need to look at where you want to be. What's your goal? Where do you want to go? Where would you really like to see yourself in life (general), love (any type of relationship) and labor (work, school, whatever)?

Don't worry about the vehicle right now—just believe you're going to get there. Believe that you belong at the end of this road. Then take action to *be* it. You can't be anything sitting still. Life, to me, is an action word. If you really want to live it, and were blessed

> *Because the truth is, everyone matters, and at some point, everyone makes a difference.*

to wake up this morning, understand there's a purpose for your life. Take action on that. You've got to see it, believe it and start being it. Be it now. See yourself as what you want to be. And then take action on it.

Our dreams are worth fighting for. Whatever the desires of your heart, don't give up on yourself. One of the greatest things you can ever do is to begin to believe in yourself. Because the truth is, everyone matters, and at some point, everyone makes a difference.

If I could go back in time and have that phone conversation with Marc, I'd tell him, "You know what? You make a difference. You can talk to anyone, you have a voice; there's so much that you have to offer this world. All you have to do is figure out what you want. People are watching you, invested in you, because they love who you are. Continue to be you. If stuff gets you down, brush it off, get up again and keep going. I've learned through trial and tribulation, my friend, that we can fail our way to success. Just don't quit."

Never give up. You can make mistakes, but mistakes don't make you. You have something within you that matters to this world. And if you haven't tapped into it, if you haven't reached in so it can come out, now is the time to do it. Tomorrow's not promised, and today is the first day of the rest of your life. Who is waiting for *your* call? Who needs you to take the first step and let *your* voice be heard? Who is waiting for you to honor *your* greatness within?

Gary Walsh, Jr., provides visionary leadership through his work as a highly sought-after speaker, trainer, ordained minister and certified life and professional coach, who specializes in personal and professional development. Gary is the President of Success in Motion, Inc,. and broadcasts his motivational message on his weekly blog talk radio program, Success In Motion Radio. *He has more than twenty years of experience in office management, finance and corporate administration for corporations such as Charles Schwab and Co., the Federal Aviation Administration, Building Bridges Foundation and The Reznick Group. Look for Gary's forthcoming book,* Dream Out Loud, *and connect with him at www.SuccessInMotionInc.com, www.Facebook. com/SuccessInMotion, and www.Twitter.com/GarySuccess.*

Linda M. Wilson

YOUR DREAM IS
YOUR OXYGEN

"Hey, look at these! These are really cool." My husband Jeff and I were sitting on the floor, sorting through big piles of old family photos to make a special album for my parents' fiftieth wedding anniversary.

Normally, Jeff pays no attention whatsoever to pictures. So I had to look. He was holding up some candid group shots from about twenty years before. The composition was great, and somehow the photographer had captured everyone as they really look. Those true expressions don't usually make it into pictures. I was so busy being impressed that it took me a minute to realize what I was seeing. Then I grinned at Jeff. "You don't even know I took those, do you?"

For a minute, I hadn't realized it either. As it sank in, I got really excited. *Hey, I'm actually good at this! Really good. I do have the eye. I do have the talent. I should just make a go of it. Who cares if it's hard? Who cares if there are ten thousand photographers in the state of Colorado already?*

Photography is like oxygen for me. I've always turned to it when I needed to get away, to release stress and to find myself. It's what I need to keep going, throughout the day; when it's a rough one and things aren't going well, I take pictures. When it's a good day, I take pictures. When I'm doing nature photography, I'm totally at peace and kind of zoned out. I often don't remember taking all the photos, or taking them the way they turned out. I feel like I'm a kind of vehicle, like I just get out there and God works through me. Photography, for me, is complete and total freedom.

I always dreamed, somewhere deep inside, of being a professional photographer. And I took pictures of *everything*—especially when my son was young. I'd take pictures first thing when I got home from work, setting up scenes in the house and playing with angles and light, or going out in the backyard and losing myself in nature. It didn't really matter what I was taking pictures of, and even if they didn't turn out very well, the whole process was very peaceful and relaxing.

I was so young when I got my first camera that I don't even remember the event, but in almost all my memories, it's me with my camera. My dad is a very talented amateur artist and

> *If you never fail, it means you've never tried anything. I didn't learn that for a long time.*

photographer, and he always gave his old cameras to my brother and me to play with. But the way I was raised, it was a hobby, not a career. Photography wasn't something grown-ups did for a living. It doesn't put food on the table.

I was afraid they wouldn't be supportive, so I never told my family that I wanted to be a photographer. Not that they were out to crush my dreams, but I grew up Catholic—*very* Catholic—and Catholics like to think about everything that can go wrong. My parents spent their lives trying to keep us from getting hurt and shielding us from failure. That approach can take away a lot of opportunity.

Because of this attitude, my father never got to live his dream. He wanted to be a physician, but he fainted at the sight of blood, so he gave up and settled for what was safe. Because he didn't get to be who he wanted to be, he surrounded himself with people who *did* do what he wanted to do. All of his best friends were doctors;

my mom was a nurse, and so were all of her friends. He even sold medical equipment for a while. Of course I learned that fear, too. I went the safe route. If you never fail, it means you've never tried anything. I didn't learn that for a long time.

When Jeff and I left the town where we both grew up, twenty years ago, we left a lot of that behind. For Jeff to pursue work in his field, we happened to move to a place where no one knew us. No one had any preconceived ideas about who we were or what

> *I stopped doubting I could do it. I was ready.*

we were supposed to do. "But you don't know anyone there!" our families said. "We know," we said. "Thank God!" It allowed us to change without any resistance. The idea of becoming a professional photographer didn't seem so crazy or unattainable anymore.

Years later, putting together my parents' anniversary album, I saw all those decades' worth of images I'd taken, stacked together like a big pile of evidence.

Not too long after that, we went to Hawaii, and I came back with an image of the Na Pali Coast that might be the best photo I've ever taken: it shows the blue of the ocean and the curvature of the earth in a kind of pure serenity. I tacked it up in my cubicle at work, and every time I wanted to push away the stress, I looked at it and it made my whole day better.

The voice inside me just refused to shut up about my awesome future life as a photographer: Utopia! My camera and I, doing whatever we want. Traveling around to all the cool places I wanted to go. Spending all my time taking pictures of the things that spoke to me. Doing it all on my own timeline, and not worrying about getting back to work at my IT job again, ever. I told Jeff, "I need to do this. It's my turn."

We started making a plan, and I began doing photo shoots as a second job so he could see how serious I was. The response to my pictures was always really positive. I stopped doubting I could do it. I was ready.

And then Jeff got sick. Really sick. An infection attacked one of his heart valves. The doctors decided they needed to perform open-heart surgery to replace the valve, but wanted to operate on healthy tissue and gave Jeff antibiotics first. I went home to bed, and when I came in early the next morning, he was dying—he had developed a staph infection. They were waiting to do surgery, but didn't think he'd survive it. A crowd of specialists swarmed around him. It was like an episode of the TV show *House*. We'd been married for almost thirty years. I couldn't stop thinking, *I'm not ready to be by myself just yet.*

Jeff survived. And then, almost eight weeks to the day later, the new valve blew in the middle of the night and they had to do another surgery.

My husband has a habit of having a major illness every ten years or so. We joke about it. "Honestly," I told him, sometime between the two surgeries, "this has to stop. It's my time. I'll wait for a year, so you can recover. I don't want you to blow another fuse. But I need to do this."

"I understand," he said. "You need to do what you need to do." Jeff is a man of few words, and I already knew I had his support. I didn't need his permission—but I did need to know he wasn't going to drop dead. I waited out one more year at my IT job, and he recovered.

It was heaven to quit my job. Aside from the negativity-drama virus that regularly swept the place (I had learned to ignore it), nothing was really wrong with my job; there just wasn't any way to combine it with my passion for photography. I swept out the door on my last day with nary a pang, went home, went out to dinner to celebrate with Jeff—and the very next morning I was on a plane to Phoenix, Arizona, headed for an assignment shooting a Bob Proctor seminar in Scottsdale. The person in the seat next to me turned to me and said, "So what do you do?"

"I'm a photographer," I said.

I'm a photographer! I can finally say that! I believed it was true for the first time, even though I'd always known. It wasn't a hobby or a side job—it was my calling. I pulled off the reply as though I'd been a professional photographer for years, and then sat there amazed, and pretty pleased with myself. My seatmate had no idea that this was the first day of the rest of my life.

If you think you're being selfish by following your dreams, you're wrong. In fact, it's selfish not to. Not only are you sending discouraging messages to your family and friends about the importance of dreams in everyone's life, but just about everyone benefits when you do what you are called to do.

My mother is a Registered Nurse specializing in geriatrics. She worked in a nursing home for years—not an easy task by any

> *We're never called to do something just for ourselves.*

means. I never understood how she could do what she did, and for so long. She's seventy-four now and retired. How does she spend her spare time? Caring for her friends that need help! It's her calling; it's what she *does*. And I am so thankful and grateful she followed her calling. She showed me it could be done. We're never called to do something just for ourselves.

When you deny that call, you're denying the world your gift. Don't wait to give your gift, and don't be afraid to fail. When you fail, you learn, and fear is a great thing to feel when you're going for your dream. In fact, if it doesn't scare the pants off of you thinking about it, it's probably not the right or the true dream. Suck it up and move on, because you'll never feel more alive than when you take that first step toward your dream and really go after it, really try to make it real.

If I hadn't taken that first step myself, I'm guessing I'd be miserable in my job, miserable in everything else, and probably making other people miserable too. Possibly I'd be divorced. Instead, I love my job and I love my life. My camera is always with me, waiting to capture an amazing moment. I couldn't have imagined how great it feels until I got here. It's something of a surprise to my parents, though; they still think I'm crazy.

Find that something that makes you feel alive—we all have it. Then pursue it with everything you've got. It's what you're here for. It's how you breathe. Don't keep it from yourself, or from the rest of us!

Linda M. Wilson, based in Denver, Colorado, speaks to audiences around the world about how photography mirrors life and business, and how changes in focus and perspective change outcomes. Linda has had a camera in her hand most of her life, and now specializes, as a professional photographer and owner of Your World Our Lens LLC, in landscape and fine art photography. Her work is featured at Grace Gallery Fine Art in Denver. Linda is at work on a book of travel tips. She is also a featured author in Loral Langemeier's forthcoming Entrepreneurial Success Stories. *Connect with Linda at www.YourWorldOurLens.com.*

Jacqueline "Jah'Key" Lucien

A View from the Mountaintop

The Race

What race are you in?
From the valley or mountain
Where do you begin?
Do you stay with the flock?
Or have vision to transcend
See that you are in the race
   of Mankind
For all to win

What race are you in?
What is your vision?
What do you comprehend?
What is the answer
To your quest i o n

Where do you end?
The answer to your question
Is where you end

Your vantage point
Determines your point of view
What you perceive, receive and do
The answer to your question
Competition or cooperation
Survival or extinction
Race, Man, Woman or Mankind
From where do you begin?
What race are you in?
Where do we end?

My hunger for knowledge began, very early, as a yearning to understand and talk with people. I was very quiet as a child. People didn't think I had anything going on because I didn't add to conversation, but there was plenty happening beneath my quiet exterior. I was busy studying and observing and gathering knowledge. "I don't know what you're studying for," my mother said to me one day. "You're not going to be anything anyway." I put my hands on my hips and said, impudently and boldly, "I know one thing—if I don't study, I'm NOT going to be anything. So I'm going to go to school and take my chances."

She also told me, "You don't have to go to school—you can get married and have kids." She had eight sisters, and those who were divorced with kids had difficulty getting support from their husbands. I looked around and said, "I ain't goin' out like that. I've got to get my *own*." The funny thing was, even back then I knew

> *I didn't listen to these voices, though they sometimes ran in the back of my head. They were trying to put me in a box I didn't belong in, and sometimes I achieved first for myself and second to prove them wrong.*

my mom wasn't seeing me clearly; she was a very bright woman seeing me through her own pain and thwarted dreams. Like the inappropriate uncle who told me later, "You're not going to finish school—you're just going to get pregnant." I didn't listen to these voices, though they sometimes ran in the back of my head. They were trying to put me in a box I didn't belong in, and sometimes I achieved first for myself and second to prove them wrong.

I was a very motivated student, and I did very well in all of my classes up until my eighth grade English class. One day, I was shocked to get a paper back with a big red "F" on it. I thought I had understood the lesson. When I compared my paper with my girlfriend's as we walked home, I saw that her paper looked just like mine. The exception was that my friend's paper was emblazoned with a big red "A."

Angry at the injustice, I stormed into the teacher's classroom and demanded to know, "Why did you give me an F?" She looked at me coldly. "Go out of this room," she said, "and come back in when you can speak to me properly." She never explained the "F," but from that point on I could never get higher than a "C" grade in her class, though I got good grades in all my other classes. In ninth grade, my eighth grade marks landed me in a lower-level

English class. Finally, in tenth grade, my teacher gave an English proficiency test. My score was perfect, and he moved me to an appropriate class.

I realized that the maneuvers by my eighth grade teacher had changed my whole school experience dramatically, and probably weakened my skills, but I never knew to what extent. The next two years were also tough, with my parents' divorce and an illness that landed my mom in the hospital. After I moved in with my grandparents, I could tell that my home life had been affecting my ability to concentrate. Fortunately, even when I was not doing well and did not know why, I never thought I was dumb. I loved information, and knew if I worked hard, I would eventually get it. So I kept plodding along.

I was accepted into San Francisco State College, and loved my classes in psychology and social work. But I was living in Berkeley,

> *I did not give up on my dream, because I felt there was no alternative but to forge ahead.*

so before I discovered a carpool, I had to take three buses nineteen miles each way to get to and from school. My mom's health crisis meant there was no financial support for me; in fact I had to help support her and pay my own tuition. I didn't know about scholarships and financial aid at the time.

Sometimes I worked so hard I couldn't keep up, and would fail a class. But I learned that it was okay to take a class over again— the next time I understood what questions to ask. My last year of college, I moved to Los Angeles, worked full time and finished at California State University, Los Angeles while attending school at night. This time it was a three-hour bus ride to school, until I asked to share a ride. I did not give up on my dream, because I felt there was no alternative but to forge ahead.

I got a job as a social worker through the state of California. During the interview process, the interviewer asked if I would like to go for a master's if I could get a stipend, which they were offering. "Yes," I said. "And I'll do whatever I have to do to make it work." I got the job, and for the next two years I did not spend my paycheck, figuring that if the state did not give me a stipend after all, I would pay for it myself.

I was accepted into the University of California, Los Angeles; the very first day of school, I headed to the learning skills center. There, I learned important skills I'd been missing, like how to speed-read, take notes and create outlines before answering test questions. Though I was pregnant with my second child during my last year of school, I graduated with a 3.85 GPA.

My teachers kept saying I didn't have to come to class, but I loved gaining information so much I didn't miss a single one. The week of graduation I was delivering a baby, and I would have had to use a wheelchair to accept my diploma, I was so weak. So instead of going to my graduation ceremony, I took pictures in my cap and gown with my son Tony, my new baby Todd in my arms, and my husband Joe.

Then, in my late thirties, I was awarded a fellowship from the prestigious Menninger Foundation, one of the top hospitals in the world. I was one of only four social workers admitted to the post-master's-degree program there, and I felt very special. Despite all the adversity, despite all of the negative messages I had received as an unvalidated child in my family and a young black woman in the educational system, I did reach the apex of my educational goals. I thought I had reached the top of the mountain.

I believe it was my gift, as a kid, to understand that even if other people had a movie of my life, even if they had already decided who I was, I didn't have to let their perceptions alter my course. I knew that if I didn't push on and fight for my dream, which was always a part of the fabric of who I am, I would wind up going crazy.

So education, for me, was a route to sanity. I had to go outside of my community, my family and the education level of my environment to get better information and to get to where I belonged.

Even after fighting off all those projections, walking around all those landmines, I'm still the child, still the idealist who wants to see the good in people, and share. I remain the eight-year-old child, maintaining my curiosity and unending desire to *know*.

I'm also looking at my own contribution to my problems more than I'm looking at anyone else. Everyone has her own projections and defense mechanisms. Erich Fromm said that whole societies can be insane. Often, when you are one of the few to perceive

> *Grab help whenever and wherever it is offered. Oftentimes, help comes from the most unlikely places: This is what I now call divine intervention. Reach out—you're not a bother. Just trust the process.*

something, society will tell you you're wrong. The whole world may tell you you're wrong, but that doesn't mean you are—you have to keep dreaming your own dream, whether it's disagreeable or challenging to others or not. You have to trust yourself, even among the "experts." Everyone has her own vantage point from which she sees. The question is, where are you? People can't see what you can see from the top of the mountain.

In addition to the negative messages, my mother taught me some wonderful lessons. "I might tell you something, and it might not be true," she told me. "You don't have to reject it, but put it on the back burner and think about it."

She also said, "You can learn from everybody. You can even learn from a fool. You can learn, at least, how *not* to be a fool." You can receive input from others with discernment, and let it incubate rather than taking it on. That's a major piece of owning your own reality. Grab help whenever and wherever it is offered. Oftentimes, help comes from the most unlikely places: This is what I now call divine intervention. Reach out—you're not a bother. Just trust the process.

We tend to want closure before it's time for closure. But openness to the ambiguity and mystery of life, and not having all the answers, is part of why you succeed in achieving your dream. The search for the answer—not the answer itself—is really what propels you on your climb to the top.

Jacqueline Lucien finished her master's degree in social work at UCLA in 1973. She was a Headstart teacher, and taught at California State Northridge. She worked as a social worker, had a private practice and became a fellow at the Menninger Foundation, earning a post-master's degree in social work in 1985. She has initiated housing programs, started a community food co-op and co-founded a major arts venue. Through her mentoring, she has contributed to the financial success of many of her peers. She also presents seminars at national conferences.

After she retired from social work, Jacqueline began to write poetry, which she frequently performs at schools and political events. She interned at a radio station and hosted her own poetry show. Later, she returned to UCLA and majored in computer graphic design. She is currently working on three books, two of which she is illustrating. Connect with Jacqueline at www.ConsiderThisToday.com.

Bill Lopez

FROM BINARY TO ANALOG: A SURVIVOR'S LONG JOURNEY

What happens to a person when he discovers that all the promises offered him by self-help books, CDs, videos and seminars are empty ones? That even through his best efforts, he can't reach a state of happiness and transcendence?

All my life, I suffered abuse. The cycle started with my parents and brothers, who abused me physically, mentally and emotionally; continued in school, with tortures at the hands of other kids; and dragged me unwillingly through an adulthood riddled with abusive relationships. Because of this, I was programmed for failure, believing that people ought to abuse me and that I could not change my life or stand up for myself. And I always sought validation as a human being from some kind of higher "authority" that never gave it to me.

My businesses and relationships failed. My income plummeted. I continued to suffer abuse at every turn. It became harder and harder to leave the house and be among other people, and I was so afraid of talking to a pretty woman that if I saw one I wanted to meet, my mouth would instantly go dry and my stomach would tie itself up in knots. I felt so terribly alone. And though I tried and tried to change, the advice and affirmations I read never rang true.

In the back of my mind, a series of automatic thoughts always piped up to say: *You're worthless. You're ugly. Everyone hates you.*

You can't do anything. I was unaware of these automatic thoughts; all I knew was that I was tired and couldn't think. This was the mechanism by which my thoughts were achieving their goal of keeping me down. It didn't matter what my intentions were—I always found myself doing the opposite.

I studied neuro-linguistic programming, hypnosis, behavioral psychology; I read the top self-help experts, and nothing was working. As I experienced crisis after crisis, I would pick up a book and think, *Maybe, at last, the answer is here.* When the promise turned out to be empty once again, it compounded my disappointment and my sense of failure. I felt an abject loneliness, and even guilt: *Why am I the guy this doesn't work for?*

And with no outer *or* inner authority to argue that the negative, automatic thoughts that directed my life were not true, I descended into a very deep, dark place. For years, my depression was so bad I couldn't sleep. My eyes burned and my body ached with exhaustion. I was in such a thick fog I could barely think. I'd get up in the morning and think, *What... do I have to... do... today...*

> *In the back of my mind, a series of automatic thoughts always piped up to say:* You're worthless. You're ugly. Everyone hates you. You can't do anything.

to get through... today? I could barely put those thoughts together, never mind thinking about my future. I was broke and a hermit, cashing in my aluminum cans just to eat. I hit my lowest point in the spring of 2004. Because I couldn't see myself moving beyond the pain, I thought a lot about suicide.

If you want to have massive success, you need to make massive personal change. For me, that massive change was a gradual process that began when I started to change my automatic thoughts, the thoughts in the back of my mind that argued with the affirmations I had learned from books. I realized that humans are not computers—go figure. We are analog, not binary, and though our thoughts may be automatic, our transformation is never instant.

The apothecary's scale of our growth is rarely weighed completely to one side or the other; we grow in increments, sometimes making great leaps but more often struggling for a while before breakthroughs begin to happen.

Out of desperation, and even in my mental fog, I did some detective work and identified the automatic thoughts running in the back of my head that had created the mechanism of failure

> *"Today I will put aside my fears, doubts, worries, insecurities and old injuries. In their place, I will focus on healing and all of the good things in my life, the people who care for me and support me, my victories, my opportunities—and, just for today, I will be energetically optimistic."*

in my life and my resistance to affirmation. Knowing what their messages were, I created my own universal affirmation to change those thoughts:

"Today I will put aside my fears, doubts, worries, insecurities and old injuries. In their place, I will focus on healing and all of the good things in my life, the people who care for me and support me, my victories, my opportunities—and, just for today, I will be energetically optimistic."

Things started to change, so I kept saying the universal affirmation.

After a while, instead of struggling in a fog every morning, I started to get up and get to work right away, checking and tweaking my eBay auctions. My income from the home business started to rise. I started riding my bike again and pursuing contact with other people. I even joined other amateur photographers at Southern California Photo Days, and made friends with some of the people I met there. Some of them are among my closest friends today.

As I mentioned before, we humans are analog, not binary. Resistance is not a block to be instantly deprogrammed. But over a relatively short period of time, my universal affirmation saved me from despair, and so saved my life. The very first night I slept through the whole night—in 2006—was a miracle.

In the past, I would always plan to go to a salsa class at a nearby nightclub, but then be so tired I'd forget about it until it was too late to go. That was my automatic thoughts in action, making me so tired I couldn't do anything. But one night, after I'd been doing my

> The number one rule is: Whatever you're affirming, the back of your mind must say a resounding yes to.

universal affirmation for a while, I was actually able to remember my plan. I started getting ready about an hour before the class, and while I was in the shower I started feeling like I was going to throw up. I was literally having a panic attack—those automatic thoughts were going to do everything they could to keep me from going out and being among people.

Rationally, I knew that if I went out and danced, I'd meet people and have a great time. But I also knew that thinking rational thoughts wasn't going to do the trick. So as I was there in the shower, I started repeating my universal affirmation over and over again. Soon, the feeling of illness started to dissipate, and my panic and anxiety levels started shifting down. So even though I was a little apprehensive when I finally left, I made it. I got there, and I had a great time. It's what I knew in my rational mind would happen, but to get there I had to overcome that anxiety and those automatic thoughts.

So why did my universal affirmation work, when every other affirmation had failed me? It worked because the back of my mind could say *yes, yes, yes* to it. The back of my mind could agree to the fact that I *did* have fears, doubts, worries, insecurities and old injuries. Because I was not denying reality, it could also handle a shift in focus in their place, and a promise that *just for today*, I could be energetically optimistic. Eventually I found that my methodology—Automatic Success™—was able to help others, too.

The number one rule is: Whatever you're affirming, the back of your mind must say a resounding *yes* to. Saying to myself, "I am energetically optimistic" would not have worked, because I just didn't believe it, just as someone who needs to lose weight and stands in front of the mirror saying, "I am thin" will argue with that statement in his subconscious mind and be unable to move forward with a program for actual weight loss and health improvement. You have to start by admitting the truth. Then you can shift your thought process, and reconnect with your purpose and your dreams.

Not everyone has the kind of journey that I made, but for anyone in pain, for anyone who has struggled to find wisdom and guidance out there and come up empty-handed, I recommend trying this: speak the universal affirmation out loud ten times in a row, three times a day. This will give you the jumpstart you need in order to shift those automatic thoughts. And as your automatic thoughts shift away from creating resistance to what you want and intend, your level of happiness and success will rise. As you shift, other compound and formatting affirmations can be created to keep shifting you to the next level.

Today, everything has changed for me. I'm out in the world, forming relationships and having fun. I make great money, vacation often and wake up happy and alert. I do my universal affirmation only occasionally these days, because I have created others that are more specifically targeted to where I am now.

Perhaps most importantly, I'm no longer identifying as a victim and asking, *Why me?* I know that the suffering, pain and turmoil I experienced were all leading me here, to a place where I can help others make massive personal change in their own lives, when once they felt no one could ever reach or help them.

Bill Lopez is the creator of a new model of psychology, Automatic Success™. Completely broken after a lifetime of abuse, Bill healed himself and transformed his life beyond what anyone thought possible. His mission is to spare others the suffering he experienced, and bring healing to those who have been hurt by others. Bill is a certified hypnotist, certified master practitioner of NLP (Neurolinguistic Programming), certified dream coach and certified spiritual group leader. He is currently writing his first book about this new model of psychology to bring healing to those who need it. Connect with Bill at www.AutomaticSuccess.net.

Sherise Patterson

RESURRECTING THE DREAM

To someone else, this might look like a big empty storefront, a giant open square with four white walls. But to me, it looks like a dream come true. In my mind's eye, I see the storefront marquee outside, bearing the name of my business in large, bright letters: *Simply to Empower*. And within the clear palette of these four walls, I see the vision I've held close for all these years: a space for empowerment, a space for all people.

Everything about the atmosphere is welcoming. In the front of the space, I see a gift shop filled with books, CDs, DVDs and other empowerment tools ranged on shelves that radiate in a friendly pattern. Near the sunny windows, I see chairs and tables set up for reading and conversation. A partition in the back of the store leads to a large, open space for events and workshops, with room to seat fifty or so community members. And in a quiet corner, I see the small sanctuary of my office.

Just a few days before, I had read the last sentences of *The Secret*, closed the book with a purposeful smile and said to myself, "This is *my* time. Let me focus on myself and finally do what I want to do." The store had been my dream for years, but I had a full-time job in addition to the full-time job of taking care of a home, and I always put my dream on the back burner.

I'm a night person, and I worked at night. So at two o'clock in the morning the very next night, my night off, I jumped in my car and started driving around my neighborhood in Queens. I was hyped: *It's time to find the home for this dream!* I turned right at my corner, then left, and there it was: a big FOR RENT sign on a storefront just blocks from my home. Even though it was the middle of the night, the sun seemed to come out right over that spot. *Wow!* I thought. *This is it! This is the Law of Attraction in action, and I didn't have to go any further than around the corner!* Once I put my dream out there, I realized it was right here, all the time.

I took down the number and went home. The next morning, I called and got the landlord on the phone. "I saw your space last night," I told him. "It's wonderful. I want to rent it." "Do you have any experience running a store?" he asked. "No," I said. "But I know this is what I really want to do." "Do you have any idea what

> *Once I put my dream out there, I realized it was right here, all the time.*

you're getting into? Do you have the money for this? Do you have the time to run a store? You know it will take over your life." The landlord kept firing discouraging questions at me, but I insisted on making an appointment to view the space.

When we hung up, all his doubting questions took root and started cycling around in my mind. But I thought, *I'm not going to listen to negative thoughts. I know I can do this, and I don't need anyone to tell me I can't.* I'd envisioned this wonderful and noble dream, and it was up to me to make it happen.

My whole life, I was told, "You can't." As a child, I was teased and humiliated for being dark-skinned, but though my legacy then was one of low self-esteem, I pressed on. In my growing years, I allowed myself to be taken advantage of. But I pressed on and learned to populate my life with loving people. As a grown woman, I lost four babies, including a pair of twins, to miscarriage. Yet, I pressed on, keeping my heart open and prayerful and using my past trials and tribulations to make me stronger.

My goal with the store was to empower the discouraged, motivate the unmotivated and bring joy to the joyless. I knew what it felt like to be on the other side of the fence, and once I'd found inner peace and happiness, I knew I could empower others to find it too. So when I walked into the space that day in 2007 and knew my dream could come to fruition there, I felt

> *My goal with the store was to empower the discouraged, motivate the unmotivated and bring joy to the joyless.*

my whole body shake with excitement. "What do you need from me?" I asked the landlord. "I'll do whatever it takes." Two days later, I brought him the rent, my deposit and a ten-page contract. He placed the keys in my hands. *You did it! You did it!* I thought. I was overjoyed.

From the moment I woke up on *Simply to Empower*'s Grand Opening day, I felt utterly joyful, like I was floating on air. I had prepared for this day for so long, and everything I envisioned had come true: the store wasn't just *like* a dream, it really *was* a dream. My dream.

I felt a wonderful sense of joy and calm as I welcomed a standing-room only crowd into *Simply to Empower*. It was a cold, gray February day, but inside it was bright and warm, packed with my family, friends and countless community members. The local radio station was there, broadcasting live. We had speakers, a comedian, even a clown handing out balloons to the kids. Everyone was happy and smiling, buying gifts and making connections. We were off to a fantastic start.

The next two years weren't easy. We were in the middle of an economic crisis, and people weren't spending money. Though I had the support of associates, family and friends, and a wonderful team, including my dear friend Cathy and my mother, Gemmel, I still wore the hats of marketer, advertiser, salesperson and owner while simultaneously working my full-time job.

But I wouldn't have changed it for the world. Though it struggled in some ways, the business was very successful because we transformed so many lives. When you stepped into *Simply to Empower,* you felt a positive aura all around you. People came to the store every day for help, and found it in the form of transformational tools, conversation, classes and fellowship. We put on transformative events, including an event at York College with Les Brown. We held business classes once a week, and I watched community members who had once struggled with huge obstacles go out and start—and grow—new businesses using solid tools. I watched lives change, every day.

And along the way I, too, learned new tools and made connections that helped me grow. New concrete friendships were made, and business relationships were built. Everybody who stepped into that space knew on some level that whatever they set out to do, they could do. And when they left, they went and did it. Watching the effect the store had on people, I knew my life was not lived in vain.

When you're operating a store, your home and doing a full-time job, you might notice some little aches and pains and think, *I'm just tired. Maybe I need a break.* I disregarded the little pain I felt in my abdomen for a while, but when I went to the doctor, I told him about it. "Don't worry," he said. "It's probably nothing. I'll run some tests." Then I got the call: "We've found a mass growing in your ovaries," he said. "Ovarian is one of the hardest types of cancer to find. I'm so sorry to tell you—yours is already at Stage Four."

You can always get your dream back, but you can't get your health back, once it's gone. Running a store is very stressful, and stress causes cancer to grow. I thought about finding someone else to run the store, but I knew that would be stressful too. I had to choose: *Your dream or your health, Sherise?* I wrestled with the decision until the very last minute. But at last I chose my health.

Handing back my keys and looking at those four white walls again was very painful, but I knew I would be back. I didn't know if I would open another store, but I *would* be back, and with a restructured dream.

As I went through chemo, surgery and recovery, I realized that my illness had given me a blessed opportunity to spread my wings, and possibly reach even more people. Because everything had changed, I was actually able to shift the business so it made more sense. Failure is not an option for me.

My dream didn't fail—I simply had to redefine, reprioritize and restructure it. When crisis derails your plans, you might think you've lost your dream, or that you have to start from scratch with a new one. But maybe that's not necessary. If you know what your mission and your purpose are, and hold fast to that knowledge, it

> *My dream didn't fail—I simply had to redefine, reprioritize and restructure it.*

doesn't have to be a failure or a loss. You can continue to build on it, with insight into some of the mistakes you may have made or some of the challenges that came up that you may never have even seen coming. Your mission can stay alive through adversity, and even grow.

When I got sick, I realized that time is not something we can afford to lose or waste. Now I'm more mindful of making every minute of my every day count and to touch as many lives as I can. Every day, we have to try to create our legacy, something worthwhile that we can give back to the planet. If people ask, "What did Sherise do? What was her legacy?" I want them to know that I didn't leave anybody out there alone. Going into this next phase of my dream, I know I have a lot of people looking at me and saying, "If she can do it, I can do it too."

If you believe in something wholeheartedly, never give up. Stay uplifted. Knock down the obstacles in your way. When, instead of bare white walls, you see the realization of a dream, run to it. And when that dream evolves, or God calls on you to be strong in the face of adversity, resurrect it. You *can* do it. And you *will*.

Sherise Patterson is a consultant and public speaker whose purpose is to empower people to take their businesses and personal lives to the next level. In 2009, New York Daily News featured her and her team in its "Spotlight on Great People" section. Sherise is also a photographer, videographer and community activist who recently retired from the New York City Transit Authority. The latest incarnation of Simply to Empower is located on Wall Street. Connect with Sherise at www.SimplyToEmpower.com.

Dr. Sheryar Masud

CLAIM YOUR TERRITORY

When I was five years old, my family moved to the United States from Pakistan. I could barely understand English, but I did understand the universal language of sports. No matter what the specific sport is—soccer, basketball, skiing—the key words in that language are the same: winning, losing, persistence, dedication, sacrifice, passion and sweat, just to name a few.

When I was seven years old, I was introduced to football. We had a friend in the neighborhood, a kid a couple of years older, and his father was a college football coach. One day, he organized us neighborhood kids for a game. The coach handed me the ball and told me what to do, and I was immediately difficult to tackle. Ever since that moment, all I wanted to do was play professional football. People said I was too small to play football, but you know the old saying: it's not the size of the man in the fight that counts, it's the size of the fight in the man.

And I had a lot of fight in me. I worked harder than everyone else around me. I was up early every morning to lift weights or run hills. When I was jogging and a car came along, I'd break into a sprint and race it. While my fellow students were off at a basketball game having fun, I was in the gym, working out and thinking about next year's game.

One of the oldest clichés in football is that it is "a game of inches." The great coach Vince Lombardi once gave a famous speech on the importance of those inches, and in it he discussed not only the inches in football but the inches in life—all those little bits here and there that add up to the big picture. The big picture that all of those inches add up to make is my territory. And my territory is a metaphor that extends to any facet of my life—my material wealth, my spiritual growth, my career, anything.

In football, your territory is obvious: it's all the grass behind you. If you're on defense, you don't want to let the opposing offense onto that grass. If you're on offense, you want to keep pushing forward, adding to your territory. I was a running back. Those

> *People said I was too small to play football, but you know the old saying: it's not the size of the man in the fight that counts, it's the size of the fight in the man.*

yards in front of me meant everything. I wanted as many of them as I could get, so much so that I was willing to do whatever I had to do to fight for every inch of them.

Through sheer hard work, I got the opportunity to play Division I football. But then disaster struck. During a game, I got a handoff, saw some daylight and sprang through the hole. I was hit once and stayed on my feet, hit a second time but still kept going. I was twenty yards downfield on the third hit when something in my knee snapped. It wasn't much later that I was on the operating table.

I had never been hurt in my life, but on that one hit I tore three of the four ligaments in one knee and also blew out my meniscus. Everything I had worked for up to that point was over in a flash. My coach broke the news to me, and I had to reevaluate my life.

For years, my mother had been telling me that I should be a doctor, and I decided she was right. I didn't want to be a medical doctor, though. Because I was so into sports, I decided I wanted to be a chiropractor. I knew the road was going to be long and expensive, but I wasn't daunted. Obstacles are God-ordained opportunities cleverly disguised as difficulties.

I spent one hundred thousand dollars and the next seven years becoming a DC (Doctor of Chiropractic). I leased a building and hung a shingle on my door, and I waited for patients to come. And waited. And waited. And they never came. So I told my friends I was going to start going door-to-door to offer my services. They said I was crazy, but I saw it as doing what I needed to do to fight for the territory of my career.

At first, it did feel crazy. People kept yelling at me, slamming doors in my face, telling me I wasn't supposed to be soliciting. But I kept knocking.

Zig Ziegler famously says that you have to go through all the noes to get to the yesses, but he didn't mention how many noes that would be. I think I must have gotten a thousand noes before I finally got a yes. But once I got that first one, the yesses just kept

> *I've always had the Kunta Kinte spirit. You can cut off my foot, but I'll still learn how to run. You can cut off my other foot, but I'll still learn how to jump and fly.*

coming. I've always had the Kunta Kinte spirit. You can cut off my foot, but I'll still learn how to run. You can cut off my other foot, but I'll still learn how to jump and fly.

Within a year, I was incredibly successful. I was earning well into six figures, I was surpassing all of my friends, and my practice management coach said I was sitting on a golden goose. But then my landlord decided not to renew my lease. Normally, that wouldn't be a big deal, but I was using all that money I'd been earning to pay off my student loans and the loans I'd needed to get my practice going. I was cash poor.

I had been young and naïve, and I had neither legal recourse regarding the lease nor money to set up shop somewhere else. I couldn't pay my bills, I couldn't pay my credit card. I lost my car and my house. Metaphorically, I'd been taken out at the knees again, and my territory was gone. I could have moved back in with my parents, but I wasn't about to do that.

I found a small clinic nobody wanted. It was shoddy, and it was in a rough neighborhood. Some kids were dealing drugs right there near the clinic. But I took it, and I fought for every inch of it. I started my practice again, and I started going door-to-door again, too. At night, I slept in the clinic, using patients' gowns for blankets. In the morning I woke up and went to the gym to pump iron. Then I felt ready to take on the day. I never saw the problems ahead of me, only the opportunities.

Business started booming again. I bought a larger clinic and moved into it, expanding my territory, and then a year later I had to buy yet another, larger, clinic. Everyone said the next clinic I

> *And I tell my patients that each of us has to have a purpose bigger than ourselves. I tell them of the difference we can make together; I tell them that if they get better, they can spread the message to other people who are sick and suffering. "It can't just be about you," I tell them.*

bought was too large, but after a year there I had to knock down some walls to expand. At one point, I was personally seeing six hundred patients a week.

But no matter how big I got, it really was always about those inches. When I'm adjusting a patient's spine, it's those inches that will make his entire body better. When a basketball player shoots the ball, she'll miss if her elbow is just an inch off from where it's supposed to be. I was taking care of my inches. While my friends bought nice cars, took vacations and spent money on themselves, I used my money to protect my ever-widening territory. I showed up at work every day and treated each patient as if he were my last. I kept a keen eye on the books and never splurged.

Eventually, my territory widened into a spiritual realm. I sensed there was a bigger purpose to what I was doing. I feel that

God made me a certain way to overcome obstacles and achieve dreams, and that I am an example to others to do the same. At my clinic, I teach about health. I inspire others to be healthy and not to quit: "It's okay to fall," I tell my patients, "but you have to keep getting back up." And I tell my patients that each of us has to have a purpose bigger than ourselves. I tell them of the difference we can make together; I tell them that if they get better, they can spread the message to other people who are sick and suffering. "It can't just be about you," I tell them.

But none of this is easy. Another one of the oldest clichés in football is, "How bad do you want this?" Frankly, that's what a lot of success comes down to. How bad do you want it? I'm a realist. Dreams aren't something you can just wish for and achieve. If you don't do what you have to do to make your dream come true, it's simply not going to.

I do believe that anyone is capable of anything—you can acquire and expand whatever territory you long for, if you work for it. But the way to acquire it, and the way to expand it, is one inch at a time. Each of us is capable of daily increments of inspiration and perspiration. But you need to get started right now, and you need to see every day as if it is the day of your dreams, because it is.

There's an indomitable spirit inside all of us that's waiting to be unleashed. You may not be able to feel it, but I can. You may not know it's there, but I do. And the way to unfurl it is inch by inch.

Dr. Sheryar Masud is a chiropractic doctor who has built his business from over one hundred thousand dollars in debt to one million dollars in collections—all with just four employees. A Les Brown platinum speaker, Sheryar is an award-winning lecturer who has been invited to speak and train at many companies, including Pella Windows, Fona International, and a multi-level marketing company that awarded him its prestigious Rising Star award. He has made many television appearances, and has his own radio show devoted to personal health. He offers a wide variety of CDs and DVDs that address health topics, sales, personal development and subconscious mind reprogramming.

Married and the father of three children, Sheryar was also given a Community Image award. To stay in shape, Sheryar, a former Division I football player, is known to push trucks for exercise. Connect with Sheryar at www.TheRealDoctor. com and on his Facebook page.

ONWARD!

Now that you have read these amazing true stories of ordinary people who made the extraordinary decision to climb out of their comfort zones and pursue their dreams, I'd like to leave some final thoughts with you.

Life is a fight for territory, and once you stop fighting for what you want, what you don't want will automatically take over. So the moment you turn the page and close this book, get started. Do something immediately. Find something that's doable. Break your goal into manageable chunks and get started. Now! With every action, with every inch, you'll gain more confidence; you'll build momentum.

Brace yourself as you pursue your dreams. Be willing to fight every step of the way, come hell or high water, even if you've lost your job, even if you don't have a dime in your pocket, even if you're afraid to answer the telephone because you're dodging creditors, even if you're going through foreclosure or you've had to file for bankruptcy, even if your spouse calls you a crazy fool and walks out on you, even if you've lost your retirement or had your health threatened.

Be willing to be uncomfortable. Be willing to go from failure to failure without giving up on yourself or your dream. Be willing to act in spite of your fears. Be willing to stand up to opposition, haters and naysayers. Be willing to hold the vision when you have no evidence to support your belief. Be willing to hang in there when everyone else has given up and thrown in the towel.

> *Be willing to be uncomfortable. Be willing to go from failure to failure without giving up on yourself or your dream.*

Encourage yourself by affirming constantly, "No matter how bad it is, or how bad it gets, I'm going to make it." Because of my own experience, I believe in my heart of hearts that if you are willing to do that, God Himself will convene angels in heaven and send them down to lend you support, and empower you to snatch victory from the jaws of defeat. All of this, because you are willing to fight for your dreams.

We invite you to experience the
Fight For Your Dreams MULTIMEDIA book.

Now that you've read these moving stories, you can also view the online version of *FIGHT FOR YOUR DREAMS* on your computer or iPad in an exciting, next-generation multimedia format.

Adding AUDIO and VIDEO conversations to the text, the co-authors share more knowledge and inspiration to help you become the champion of your own life.

We offer you a GIFT of several chapters from the *Fight For Your Dreams* multimedia book at:

www.Fight4YourDreams.com

If you wish to buy the complete multimedia book, please use this coupon code to receive a substantial discount.

Coupon Code — Book6

We welcome you to experience other Yinspire Media bestselling books, available in both print and multimedia editions. Read and experience several free chapters of each multimedia book, with our compliments. If you wish to buy a complete multimedia book, use the coupon codes to receive a substantial discount.

Living Proof
Celebrating the Gifts that Came Wrapped in Sandpaper
www.LivingProofMBook.com

Coupon Code – Book5

How Did You Do That!
Stories of Going for IT
www.HowDidUDoThat.com

Coupon Code – Book2

The Law of Business Attraction
Secrets of Cooperative Success
www.LawOfBusinessAttraction.com

Coupon Code – Book1

Transforming Through 2012
Leading Perspectives on the New Global Paradigm
www.2012MultimediaEbook.com

Coupon Code – Book 4

The Wealth Garden
The New Dynamics of Wealth Creation in a
Fast-Changing Global Economy
www.WealthGardenBook.com

Coupon Code – Book 3

You can purchase the print versions of these books at Amazon.com

We also invite you to share your thoughts about our books with our community on our Facebook page at:

www.YinspireMediaFacebook.com